ACCLAIM FOR RICHARD GREENBERG'S

THE VIOLET HOUR

"Haunting . . . *The Violet Hour* is a well-crafted play filled
with wonder, a celebration of possibility and anticipation of
things to come." —MICHAEL KUCHWARA, ASSOCIATED PRESS

"[A] beguiling . . . time-machine tragicomedy [filled with]
restless, gorgeously written observations about life, love and
literati." —LINDA WINER, *NEWSDAY*

"Theatergoers who lament the absence of original American
plays should make a point of seeing *The Violet Hour* . . .
The wonder of *The Violet Hour* is how it melts from
clever, fantastical period pastiche into a poignant and
profound portrait of how time ultimately makes fools of
everyone, even visionaries determined to control their own
legends." —BEN BRANTLEY, *THE NEW YORK TIMES*

"A chamber piece that muses on the elusive intersections
between the past, the present and the future . . . Greenberg
has concocted an ingenious time-travel story with a novel
twist." —CHARLES ISHERWOOD, *VARIETY*

"Eloquent . . . This is Greenberg in his prime, witty but seriously saying something about the way we think. *The Violet Hour* has a lot of swanky, carefully crafted language to recommend it." —MICHAEL PHILLIPS, *CHICAGO TRIBUNE*

"Greenberg remains one of the few writers of his generation whose passion for language and ideas is matched by an overriding sense of good will." —ELYSA GARDNER, *USA TODAY*

RICHARD GREENBERG

THE VIOLET HOUR

RICHARD GREENBERG is the author of *Take Me Out* (Tony, New York Drama Critics Circle, Drama Desk, Outer Critics Circle, Drama League, and Lucille Lortel awards); *The Dazzle* (Outer Critics Circle Award; Lucille Lortel and Gassner nominations); *Three Days of Rain* (Los Angeles Drama Critics Award; Olivier, Drama Desk, and Hull-Warriner nominations); *Everett Beekin*; *Hurrah at Last*; *Night and Her Stars*; and *The Extra Man*, among many other plays. His adaptation of Strindberg's *Dance of Death* was staged on Broadway starring Ian McKellen, Helen Mirren, and David Strathairn. He received the Oppenheimer Award for a debuting playwright and the first Pen/Laura Pels Award for a playwright in midcareer, and has twice been a finalist for the Pulitzer Prize. Mr. Greenberg is a longtime member of the Ensemble Studio and an associate artist at the South Coast Repertory.

ALSO BY RICHARD GREENBERG,

AVAILABLE FROM FABER

Take Me Out

The Dazzle and *Everett Beekin*

THE
VIOLET
HOUR

THE VIOLET HOUR

A PLAY BY **RICHARD GREENBERG**

FABER AND FABER, INC.

An affiliate of FARRAR, STRAUS AND GIROUX / NEW YORK

FABER AND FABER, INC.
An affiliate of Farrar, Straus and Giroux
19 Union Square West, New York 10003

Distributed in Canada by Penguin Books of Canada Limited
Printed in the United States of America
FIRST EDITION, 2004

Library of Congress Cataloging in Publication Data
Greenberg, Richard, 1958–
    The violet hour / by Richard Greenberg.— 1st ed.
      p.   cm.
    ISBN 0-571-21184-4 (pbk. : alk. paper)
      1. Triangles (Interpersonal relations)—Drama.   2. Publishers and
publishing—Drama.   3. New York (N.Y.)—Drama.   4. Time travel—Drama.
I. Title.

    PS3557.R3789V56 2004
    813'.54—dc22

                                                        2003021584

Designed by Gretchen Achilles

www.fsgbooks.com

10   9   8   7   6   5   4   3   2   1

THE VIOLET HOUR

THE VIOLET HOUR was originally commissioned by the South Coast Repertory (David Emmes, producing artistic director; Martin Benson, artistic director), where it received its world premiere on November 8, 2002. It was directed by Evan Yionoulis; sets were designed by Christopher Barreca; costumes by Candice Cain; lighting by Donald Holder; with original music and sound design by Mike Yionoulis. The production stage manager was Jamie A. Tucker. The cast was as follows:

GIDGER	*Mario Cantone*
ROSAMUND PLINTH	*Kate Arrington*
DENIS McCLEARY	*Curtis Mark Williams*
JESSIE BREWSTER	*Michelle Hurd*
JOHN PACE SEAVERING	*Hamish Linklater*

The Violet Hour was subsequently produced by the Steppenwolf Theatre Company (Martha Lavey, artistic director; Michael Gennaro, executive director) on April 17, 2003, at the Steppenwolf Mainstage Theatre in Chicago, Illinois. It was directed by Terry Kinney; sets were designed by Robert Brill; costumes by Mara Blumenfeld; lighting by James F. Ingalls; with sound design and composition by Michael Bodeen and Rob Milburn. The production stage manager was Laura D. Glenn. The cast was as follows:

3

GIDGER	*Tim Hopper*
ROSAMUND PLINTH	*Kate Arrington*
DENIS McCLEARY	*Kevin Stark*
JESSIE BREWSTER	*Ora Jones*
JOHN PACE SEAVERING	*Josh Hamilton*

The New York premiere took place on November 6, 2003, at the Biltmore Theatre. It was produced by the Manhattan Theatre Club; Lynne Meadow, artistic director, and Barry Grove, executive producer. It was directed by Evan Yionoulis; sets were designed by Christopher Barreca; costumes by Jane Greenwood; lighting by Donald Holder; sound by Scott Myers; and special effects design by Gregory Meeh. The production stage manager was Ed Fitzgerald. The cast was as follows:

GIDGER	*Mario Cantone*
ROSAMUND PLINTH	*Dagmara Dominczyk*
DENIS McCLEARY	*Scott Foley*
JESSIE BREWSTER	*Robin Miles*
JOHN PACE SEAVERING	*Robert Sean Leonard*

SETTING

John Pace Seavering's office and its anteroom in a Manhattan tower. April 1919. Early afternoon to early evening.

CHARACTERS

JOHN PACE SEAVERING—*mid-twenties*
DENIS McCLEARY—*mid-twenties*
JESSIE BREWSTER—*forty to fifty*
ROSAMUND PLINTH—*early- to mid-twenties*
GIDGER—*ageless*

ACT ONE

The office.

Doors upstage through which can be glimpsed an anteroom.

A window that affords a prospect of the city.

The office is not yet set up. A desk or table, some chairs. Stacks of manuscripts. Loose paper. Clutter.

JOHN *and* GIDGER *are searching for something tiny.*

GIDGER Paper! Miles and miles and miles of paper! Sheaves and reams and passels and stacks! Is this what I went to college for? Is this why I learned sonnet form (Shakespearean AND Petrarchan thank you very much), and became proficient and gifted and wise beyond my years, and studied Latin AND glanced at Greek, and memorized the lymphatic system and kingdom-phylum-class-order-family-genus-species (K.P.C.—Oh for goodness' sake) and honed my wit and read Edmund Burke and translated sententiae from Catullus AND studied Titian and Caravaggio and da Vinci AND took a lesson in flute or flaut AND abided by Mens Sana Corpore

Sano even when it would have been just as nice NOT to wash or to entertain an impure thought so I could be inundated AND embargoed and generally assaulted by paper paper, pillars and columns and towers of PAPER?

JOHN It's not *that* messy, Gidger—

GIDGER Oh, Mr. John Pace Seavering—

JOHN Have you found the tickets?

GIDGER Found the tickets? FOUND the tickets? We're searching for a proverbial needle in a real HAYstack—

JOHN This is the way a new office is supposed to look—

GIDGER If your mother could see what this place—if MY mother could see what this place—

JOHN Why is the needle proverbial and the haystack real?

GIDGER Are you trying to sidetrack me into LITerature?

JOHN I'm just picking up on your own figure.

GIDGER No, Mr. John Pace Seavering, I AM sorry, but I cannot search and lecture at one and the same time. For you to understand my "figure," as you so pedantically call it, you would have to undertake a course of Asiatic studies lasting—

JOHN *Damn* it! Where does one put theater tickets?

GIDGER That depends. What's the play?

JOHN *Faintly My Heart.*

(GIDGER *looks at him, picks up wastepaper basket, searches in there.*)

Oh, it's an enormous hit.

GIDGER And we know what "hit" rhymes with, don't we?

JOHN Everyone I've spoken to—

GIDGER Well they're WRONG!

　　It's UTterly predictable. Predictablepredictable-
predictable. You know what's going to happen from the
SECond the maid enters with the bowl of roses—

JOHN Tickets are impossible to come by; when did you even
see it?

GIDGER *See* it? Oh, I have no interest in seeing it. Seeing it
might get in the way of my opinion.

JOHN *(affectionately)* How do the Arts survive with *you*
watching them?

GIDGER *(stops, looks at him not so affectionately)* . . .

JOHN Uh . . . what I mean is—

GIDGER Have you read what I gave you?

JOHN . . . What you gave me . . .

GIDGER Yes. What I gave you.

JOHN Well, I've been—

GIDGER Yes, I see.

JOHN I gave it a glance, of course—

GIDGER A "glance."

JOHN No, not so much a glance, really.

　　I *peered* at it.

GIDGER And what did you think?

JOHN I liked it very much.

GIDGER Which did you prefer?

JOHN I liked *them* very much.

GIDGER The free verse or the sonnet?

JOHN . . . Well, of course, I favor free verse these days, but—

GIDGER IT WAS PROSE!

JOHN They were?

GIDGER IT was. IT was! A single piece of flowing prose of which your total ignorance does NOT prevent you from forming an opinion of TWO POEMS!

How do the Arts survive with you *peering* at them?

JOHN I'm so sorry, Gidger, I'm awfully busy these days. Hang out your shingle in this publishing game and—well— *(indicating room)* Look what happens—

GIDGER What is this farce we're playing?

JOHN . . . Beg pardon?

GIDGER What am I to you, Mr. Seavering?

JOHN . . . My employee.

GIDGER And what does that mean, exactly?

JOHN . . . I tremble in your presence.

GIDGER As well you should, as well you should.

JOHN *(a charming smile)* Oh, come on, old man, ease up a bit.

GIDGER I am your employee in a business that does not exist.

JOHN How can you say it doesn't exist? Look around you. What do you see?

GIDGER PAPER!

JOHN And that's the realest thing there is.

GIDGER What have you published?

JOHN . . . Oh, Gidger . . .

GIDGER Nonono! Tell me. Recite your *list*.

JOHN . . . My list is blank.

GIDGER "My List Is Blank." Mm. Title for your MEMoirs, perhaps?

JOHN Everyone starts somewhere—

　　　　　　　　　　　　　　　　RICHARD GREENBERG

GIDGER I am the flunky of a man with a messy office: that is me in toto.

JOHN Gidger—

GIDGER You are not personal with me, and you are not PROfessional with me. We are NOTHING to each other.

JOHN I hold you in very high esteem, Gidger.

GIDGER Is Gidger my first name or my last?

JOHN . . . Pardon?

GIDGER I said: IS GIDGER MY FIRST NAME OR MY LAST?

JOHN Why . . . it never occurred to me it was either.

It never occurred to me it was your *name* at all.

I thought it was just . . . what we called you.

. . .

Sort of . . . in *lieu* of a name.

(GIDGER turns away; hissy fit.)

How *are* you?

GIDGER I beg your—?

JOHN I said: How are you?

GIDGER . . . You mean physically?

JOHN . . . Yes, all right, yes.

GIDGER Because of my *mental* state, I've given you a fair account.

JOHN Yes, then, yes: how are you physically?

GIDGER . . . Not bad.

And you?

JOHN Quite well, thank you.

. . .

How's your dog?

GIDGER Despicable.

JOHN *Is* he?

GIDGER Yes.

JOHN That sweet thing?

GIDGER A low, irredeemable creature.

JOHN I'm sure not.

GIDGER DON'T CONTRADICT ME.

JOHN I wouldn't.

GIDGER He is ut-ter-ly lack-ing in the quality of EMpathy.

JOHN No!

GIDGER Every night it's the same thing. I return home to my
garret after my day of . . . *this* . . . and I ask him,
dutifully, Would you like to be walked?

And INVARIABLY he replies: Yes, I would like very
much to be walked.

Never ONCE does he inquire as to whether I really
FEEL like walking him. Never ONCE has he picked up on
my mood.

Would you like to be walked?

Yes, I would like very much to be walked.

Garish mandibles dripping leash.

Tail swishing like a bobbin, like a SHUTtlecock, the
long-sought machine of perpetual motion.

Would you like to be walked?

Yes, I would like very much to be walked.

Would you like to be fed?

Yes, I would like very much to be fed.

Well, maybe I DON'T FEEL LIKE IT!

Maybe I need a DRINK and a FOOT RUB!

RICHARD GREENBERG

Nono!

Would you like to be walked?

Yes, I would like very much to be walked.

Would you like to be fed?

Yes, I would like very much to b—

A DOG'S LIFE? You know who leads a dog's life?

A DOG'S MASTER.

I'm going to have him killed.

JOHN You're *not*—

GIDGER I'm seriously considering it.

JOHN You wouldn't kill— What's his name?

GIDGER Sir Lancelot. But sometimes I call him Lance and
sometimes I call him Sir. Sometimes I call him Lancie,
sometimes I call him La. Sometimes I call him Celot,
sometimes I call him Slut. Sometimes I call him Lut
sometimes I call him Sla sometimes I call him Ut. With
each new name, I HOPE to call forth some as yet
undiscovered and admirable aspect of his personality.

(shakes his head sharply, a definite punctuation)

JOHN *(mildly)* You're not going to kill your puppy.

GIDGER *(the anguish of the powerless)* Can't I even kill my
dog?

JOHN No.

GIDGER What do I *have*?

I live in *Queens*!

JOHN We need to find those tickets.

GIDGER *Choke* on them!

(DENNY enters.)

DENNY Hello, Pace, I'm early.

JOHN Hi, Denny. When were you due?

DENNY Oh—I don't know—hours from now. I couldn't wait.

GIDGER Mr. Denis —one "N": the Irish—McCleary is here, Mr. Seavering. He's burst in, unannounced, brash like all his tribe, *hours* in advance of his appointment. Just in case you actually believed this was a REAL office.

(GIDGER exits.)

DENNY That fellow's highly strung.

What are you all dithering about?

JOHN I'm looking for something—

DENNY You don't mind that I'm here.

JOHN No no—look at this place—we don't stand on ceremony—
        (indicating chair) Sit—sit.

DENNY On these theater tickets?

JOHN Oh.

DENNY What's the play?

(inspects the tickets)

        Oh.

(hands them to JOHN as though they smell bad)

JOHN I'm told it's first rate. ——

DENNY Don't be ridiculous.

JOHN I'm not being—

DENNY The American theater will never achieve anything like a European maturity until I turn my attention to plays.

JOHN Oh God, is that imminent?

DENNY Why are you wasting your time on the *theater*?

JOHN It's not such a peculiar thing to—all sorts of people go to the—*these* tickets were hard to get—

DENNY It's not "all sorts" of people that go to the theater, it's one sort of people, *one* sort who like to *con*sort with *their* sort—

JOHN Oh Denny, don't say stuff like that; it's nauseating—

DENNY The really *big* problem with the Broadway theater today is you always know what's going to happen. Why pay attention when you can tell how something's going to end? In my work, the reader will never know where the story's headed.

JOHN Why give him that advantage over the author?

DENNY What?

JOHN What do you think of this place?

DENNY *(looks around)* . . . Hovel.

JOHN It's a wee bit messy.

DENNY What are all these pages everywhere?

JOHN It's the funniest thing, Denny: I call myself a publisher, and people *believe* it. They send me things . . .

DENNY *(insecure) Other* people do?

JOHN Yes!

   (appeasing) Unsolicited things, you know, nothing to . . . Why aren't you at work?

DENNY . . . Work?

JOHN These are working hours, aren't they?

DENNY . . . I dunno.

   I s'pose.

JOHN . . . Denny?

DENNY The thing about being one rung above ruin is, it's not much better than ruin.

JOHN You haven't—?

DENNY In fact, it's a little worse, because you always have the *specter* of ruin hovering about everywhere.

JOHN Denny, you can't quit your job.

DENNY Actually . . . I can.

JOHN Not *again*—

DENNY In life, Pace, you have to either soar or plummet; it's this vast *in between* that destroys the soul.

(GIDGER enters.)

GIDGER Excuse me. May *I* speak, or are you too busy exchanging essays and aphorisms?

JOHN Speak, Gidger.

GIDGER This machine has come.

JOHN What machine?

GIDGER A. ma. chine.

JOHN Did we order a machine?

GIDGER Oh, are we "we" all of a sudden? Have I exECutive authority? Can I disMISS people?

JOHN What sort of machine is it?

GIDGER Indecipherable.

JOHN Is it large?

GIDGER I should say so: "large."

JOHN Does it do something . . . make toast or something?

GIDGER Well, I don't know—why not let's test it out, have you some slices of BREAD on you?

DENNY Could it be a telegraph machine?

*(*GIDGER *looks at* DENIS, *turns to* JOHN.*)*

GIDGER Would you like to take a look?

JOHN A little later, Gidger, I have something to deal with
here.

GIDGER . . .

Ah.

. . .

(He exits.)

DENNY What could it be?

JOHN Who knows? These merchants sell you things, you
listen with one ear . . .

Denny, you have to get your job back.

DENNY I can't, Pace.

JOHN Why not?

DENNY I said some things . . .

JOHN *Why?*

DENNY I don't know.

JOHN Denny, Denny . . .

DENNY Well yes, I do, I think. I think I said them to make
going back impossible.

JOHN You idiot.

DENNY Sometimes you have to do that, you have to make
things irreversible so as not to be stuck in reverse—

JOHN It wasn't such a bad job.

DENNY You didn't do it.

JOHN No, I didn't.

DENNY It's very wrong of you, Pace, to tell me what I "must"
do and "need" do when your own life is devoid of
"musts," of "need"—

JOHN I *worry* about you—

DENNY Then you shouldn't worry about my leaving that
job—you should worry about my staying—

JOHN Everybody has jobs like that at the start—you're
young—

DENNY I'm *an*cient—I've already begun to *ox*idize—

JOHN Denny—

DENNY I was writing slogans for dry cleaners!

My talent was oozing away by the hour!

Pace, it's already the first of April 1919, the world's the
oldest it's ever been, and I'm *nothing*.

JOHN What will you *do*? What will happen to you?

DENNY You tell me: what will?

(Pause.)

JOHN Ah.

DENNY Have you at least *read* it?

JOHN . . . Yes. Yes, I have.

(Pause.)

DENNY Silence is so immensely cruel. What did you *think*?

JOHN Well . . .

(He strokes his chin thoughtfully.)

DENNY Torpid, senile, twenty-five-year-old wretch, SPEAK!

(JOHN pulls a large packing carton towards himself.)

JOHN I liked this section very much . . .

DENNY Yes? Yes?

*(JOHN pulls another similar-sized carton towards
him.)*

JOHN Around here, the story grew vague . . .

DENNY I quite agree . . .

RICHARD GREENBERG

(JOHN, *with some effort, pulls towards him a carton half again as large as the others.*)

JOHN And this part, don't you think—?

DENNY Oh, absolutely!

JOHN But all in all—

DENNY Are you going to publish it?

JOHN . . . In its present form, I don't have quite enough capital to cover the costs of the paper.

DENNY But in its future form?

JOHN Who knows what that is?

DENNY I do—*you* do if you think about it!

JOHN Also, there's some pretty rough stuff in here—for instance, this section on what you call, alternately, Materna Dentata and Matrix Dentata—

DENNY I wasn't sure which was the correct Latin—

JOHN Latin doesn't enter into it anywhere—it's the *content* that I'm—

DENNY We live in a hopelessly effeminate culture. Until we overthrow the Mother and reinstate the Father, Western civilization will not advance one whit—

JOHN Yes, well, everyone accepts that, but still this . . . grotesque image of the teeth coming out of the mother's *(clears his throat)* womb—

DENNY That is a literal portrait of my mother in Indiana, John.

JOHN No it isn't . . .

DENNY Have you *met* her?

JOHN Either way, it could get us thrown into jail before we've even—

DENNY *Yank* it, then—it's ten pages out of two million—

JOHN Which brings us back to the first problem—

DENNY Does it excite you?

JOHN . . . Yes.

DENNY Well, then.

JOHN But Denny, right now you can't even call it a novel. It's more a sort of anthology.

DENNY My aims aren't narrow.

JOHN "Aim" has nothing to do with it. You don't really "aim" at all; you more sort of strafe.

DENNY I believe in the novel of inclusion. In the argument between Wells and James, I'm a decided Wellsian.

JOHN You're more McClearyan than either, and that's not yet a finished thing. This isn't a novel, it's a . . . grouping of pages, not even a *pile*, you need one of those vivid words they use for birds and cats—a gaggle of—a murder—a ca*tas*trophe of pages! Not a single thing at all, but this vast, unedited, unorganized, untitled—

DENNY It has a title!

JOHN . . . Oh yes?

DENNY Yes. As of a few days ago. Twilight a few days ago.

JOHN *(amused) Twi*light a few days ago.

DENNY Yes.

JOHN And what would that title be?

DENNY "The Violet Hour."

JOHN *(tastes it)* . . . "The Violet Hour" . . .

DENNY *(tentative, proud)* Yes.

JOHN . . . A little swish?

DENNY No!

RICHARD GREENBERG

JOHN *(overlaps)* No, I like it.

DENNY It's that time—that wonderful New York hour when the evening's about to reward you for the day—

JOHN Yes—that light—

DENNY The violet light you walk between that hastens you places . . .

JOHN . . . Yes.

It's nice.

DENNY *Will* you publish it?

JOHN Denny, it's about twenty-five books—

DENNY No, it has a title. Once a thing has a title, it's single.

JOHN That's nuts.

DENNY That's a basic taxonomic principle!

JOHN Do you have *any* real information? Is everything you know made up?

DENNY Why *won't* you publish it—

JOHN I haven't said I won't—I'm not sure that I *can*! Economically.

DENNY . . . Why is it only the rich who never have money to do things?

JOHN I'm—

DENNY I'll tell you why: it's because the poor are always seeking opportunities, while all the rich want are limitations. You're terrified by the vastness of what's available to you, so you devote yourself to these fictional constraints which, being unreal, are insuperable. And who suffers for it? *I* do!

JOHN I'm just starting out. If I publish your book, I could lose my shirt—

DENNY But then you'll have your sweater . . . and your
coat . . . and all your other shirts.

JOHN The money isn't mine—the money is not *yet* mine—it
hasn't come down to me; a *pitt*ance has, that's all. I'm
just starting out here. I may not be—I may not have the
ca*pac*ity to publish more than one book . . . to start.

DENNY I tell you: it *is* one book!

JOHN That's not what I mean.

DENNY Then what do you—
(dawns on him)
      No.

JOHN There is another book I'm . . . there is another book
under consideration.

DENNY Another book?
How could there be another book?
Mine is the *only book necessary.*

JOHN Oh, Denny.

DENNY Mine is a *last text.*
It's like *Leaves of Grass.* After reading my book,
people won't need to read any more, they'll *live.*

JOHN It's my impression that people continued to read even
after *Leaves of Grass*—

DENNY Don't pin the failures of Walt Whitman on me, John—
(JOHN *laughs.*)

DENNY What *is* this "other book"? Who wrote it?

JOHN —I don't want to say— I don't want to expose this . . .
innocent bystander to your venom—

DENNY Is it Trippy?

JOHN No.

DENNY Are you publishing *Trippy*'s book over *mine*?

JOHN No.

DENNY Or Kefauver or Vance or *Hart*wick?

JOHN *God*, no—life is bigger than college, you know.

DENNY No it isn't—it's smaller.

JOHN It's no one from school.

DENNY . . . What other people do you *know*?

JOHN I travel in circles you can't imagine.

(Beat.)

DENNY Funny, isn't it, how all relationships turn into struggles for power?

JOHN Nonsense.

DENNY "Nonsense"! Yes, I know that word—you *taught* me that word. It means: "Exactly right, but we needn't raise our voices."

JOHN Oh what a crock—

DENNY Princeton—strangely—was much more democratic than this shabby little room. You had money—I had talent. You had family—I had personal magnetism. It balanced out. If anything *tipped* to my favor. Less generous observers might consider this a sort of revenge—

JOHN Denis.

There is something at stake for *me* here as well.

I feel—I *know*—that this could be an important thing I'm starting. I don't want to misstep.

DENNY . . . You know what your trouble is, John?

You have no spirit of ruin . . .

JOHN No, I haven't.

DENNY That's a terrible thing, Pace—that's the *defining* trait of a mediocrity,—

JOHN I don't want to be ruined.

DENNY You *should* want it—the world wants it for you. To be ruined and reconstructed and ruined again—that's life.

JOHN Not my life.

DENNY *(anguished)* You have to publish this, you see, or else it's all over.

JOHN It's all right to be down-and-out in your twenties—

DENNY You don't understand—

JOHN —I know it feels urgent—

DENNY You don't understand—

JOHN —but it's just experience.

DENNY There's a woman.

(GIDGER enters.)

GIDGER The machine is making a noise.

JOHN What sort of noise?

GIDGER Tick-tick-tick-tick-tick-tick-tick-tick-tick.

JOHN . . . Did you flip a switch?

GIDGER No.

JOHN What did you do?

GIDGER Nothing.

JOHN Then why is it going tick-tick-tick-tick-tick-tick-tick-tick-tick?

GIDGER *I* don't know.

(Beat.)

JOHN Well, I'm sure it's just something.

(Beat.)

RICHARD GREENBERG

GIDGER Do you want to come *look*?

JOHN A bit later.

(GIDGER *looks at him, then at* DENNY. *Exits.*)

JOHN What's her name?

DENNY Rosamund.

JOHN Rosamund. Yes, it would be. Rosamund what?

DENNY Plinth.

JOHN . . . Plinth? . . . Of the meatpacking Plinths?

DENNY That's the father.

JOHN *(suppressing laughter)* So she's . . . the meat heiress?

DENNY American fortunes often have absurd roots, there's no need to—

JOHN How does she look? Is she beefy?

DENNY You're being a—child—

JOHN *(laughing hard)* Where did you meet her—in the Tenderloin?

DENNY I met her at a party, and she's exquisite beyond anything I've ever seen.

JOHN Oh—

DENNY And she's got gifts beyond belief—she sings, and dances, and paints like a dream.

And I *love* her.

JOHN . . . You love her money—

DENNY The way she laughs!

JOHN Oh dear God!

DENNY I know that sounds like fiction for ladies—

JOHN So much of what you write does—

DENNY But I mean so much more—

JOHN It doesn't come through yet.

DENNY It will in later drafts!

JOHN . . . Her . . . *laugh*, then.

DENNY It's tiered.

JOHN As in lachrymose?

DENNY As in *levels*.

JOHN Oh: "tiered."

DENNY When you first hear it, it seems utterly inadvertent, like an accident happening in another room, and then it's there, suddenly, next to you, and you think of water—of a brook you've stumbled upon on a ramble. Then you realize it's none of that, it's nothing so common, it's not something you can sense at all—what it really is is a kind of intelligence. Calling attention to itself. The chime of a mind . . . a bell . . . the *toll* of intelligence. Wise and slightly sad, with history in it—

JOHN That must be some laugh—

DENNY It is—

JOHN I hope she doesn't do it too often—there wouldn't be time for conversation—

DENNY It—

JOHN Or to eat—

DENNY It's only a few notes.

JOHN And you hear all that in it?

DENNY Because all that *is* in it.

She's mine, Pace. She's meant to be mine.

JOHN . . . Are these things ever really inevitable? Or is that just the way we interpret them? The gloss?

RICHARD GREENBERG

DENNY You can't understand because you don't live your life
that way, but it's true.

Things have happened. There've been . . . proofs.

JOHN Proofs?

(Beat.)

Really?

DENNY With that kind of girl . . . these things count.

JOHN How did *that* happen?

DENNY One afternoon . . . she took me to her home . . .

JOHN To Chicago? She took you to Chicago?

DENNY Not Chicago. New York. Fifth Avenue.

JOHN Ah—the pied-à-terre.

DENNY Yes—the pied-à-terre—

It was on the gazillionth floor —

JOHN The pied-à-ciel . . . !

DENNY Yes—the pied-à-ciel!

She led me through all these rooms . . . there were so
many rooms . . . all these rooms to her room . . . like a
trail, a famous trail, I thought there must be a *map*, this
is one of those inevitable rooms that pioneers discover—

JOHN You're overwriting again.

DENNY I couldn't believe it was happening—with this kind of
girl! I didn't know what was what—I forgot everything I'd
ever known!

It was as if I weren't myself. As if I'd become the girl.

JOHN Christ, Denny.

DENNY And then it happened and I felt married to her.

(Pause.)

JOHN And *then*?

DENNY *(puzzled)* . . . Then?

JOHN Yes.

DENNY There was no "then," John.

JOHN There *was*, Denny. I know there was because you're here now.

DENNY . . . I'm not sure what you're asking for.

JOHN The moment when everything turned rotten and your prose improved.

DENNY *(Beat.)*

I don't want to go into that.

JOHN But *do*.

DENNY . . .We'd fallen asleep. When I woke up, she was gone. It was as if—

JOHN Hold off on the similes for a moment—

DENNY . . . My body ached; there was a sewer taste in my mouth, and I was ravenous. The whole world seemed to—

JOHN *(bringing him back to earth)* So you got dressed.

DENNY . . . Yes. And made my way into the street. It had rained, and the rain had given way to a milky kind of sun; the day was humid and I could smell myself, something rank. I walked until I found an Automat where, with the last few pennies I'd have for two days, I bought a sandwich. I sat down, and within seconds a bum sat across from me. Truly, it seemed that all of life—

JOHN Any particular kind of bum?

DENNY All bums are the same, John.

JOHN Not really.

DENNY . . . He had only two teeth, one perfect and one snaggled.

JOHN There you are.

DENNY And he ate a soup made of hot water and mustard. And I gobbled my sandwich down and bared my teeth so he could see *I* was eating *meat*.

JOHN And then?

DENNY He asked if I'd like a little of his soup.

JOHN And you fled.

DENNY And I—*fled*—!

JOHN And you thought—

DENNY And I thought:

This is what's waiting; the rest is unreal.

JOHN But then—

DENNY But then I saw that it had rained again, lightly, and the rain had cooled the air and puddled the street with these tiny, skittish oil paintings, and I wasn't hungry anymore, and my body didn't ache, and I thought yes—

and I thought *no*—

and I thought *yes*—

Rosamund had happened.

Then clerks and secretaries started to emerge from office buildings and scurry every which way and the daylight dimmed and the neon lights switched on and people's reflections dappled in store windows and I thought: This is the violet hour!

And I thought: *That's* my title!

And for the first time that day, I was altogether present. I had no money—I would have to walk home over the Queensborough Bridge, but I didn't despair as I usually did because I knew—I *knew*—I would only be crossing this bridge a few more times, and suddenly I was inside my horrible little apartment. I stripped naked and got into bed and melted to sleep and slept seventeen hours and next day I arrived at work four hours late and showered my boss with obscenities.

(Pause.)

So you see, you *have* to publish me, or my happiness is ended.

JOHN I don't see that at all. If she loves you—

DENNY *John!*

*(*JOHN *looks up;* DENNY, *then, quite softly and seriously)*

You invented the world—why don't you know how it works?

JOHN . . . If she *loves* you—

DENNY There's a father—and a fellow in the Midwest— agreements had been made between them before I ever came onto the scene—a man named Armitage—

JOHN Of the breweries?

DENNY Yes.

There's some hope of consolidating the family interests—

JOHN Steak and ale, oh my word—

DENNY Yes.

You see, the whole gizmo's already started up—I have to bring at least a *promise* of something, or . . . doom.

JOHN Yes, I see.

(Beat.)

I love the book, of course.

DENNY Yes . . . ?

JOHN I love it . . . them—*it*—

DENNY Oh, Pace—

JOHN It will—would be a gigantic task, of course—bringing it into line—

DENNY Then you're going to—

JOHN I didn't say that—

DENNY But you're inclined—

JOHN In*clined*—

DENNY Wait till you meet her!

JOHN Who?

DENNY Rosamund.

JOHN When?

DENNY In just a few minutes—

JOHN What?

DENNY She's coming here—

JOHN Why?

DENNY To clinch it—

JOHN Denny— I still need time—to—

DENNY It's done! It's done! It's a deal!

Oh, I *adore* you!

(DENNY grabs JOHN's head and kisses him passionately on the mouth.)

(JESSIE BREWSTER enters.)

JESSIE Am I early?

JOHN Miss Brewster!

JESSIE The fellow in the other room who does the introductions . . .

JOHN No no no . . .

JESSIE He was talking to an invention . . .

JOHN I think you're right on—

JESSIE You can call me when you're ready.

(She exits.)

DENNY And who was *that* Ethiopian apparition?

JOHN Hush!

DENNY She *was* colored, right?

JOHN Will you please lower your voice?

It's Jessie Brewster—

DENNY Jessie Brewster?

She's the famous colored singer, right? The one with the strange style? The one who ululates?

JOHN . . . Yes.

DENNY How the hell do you know her from?

JOHN *(improvising)* She has this painting . . . I'm thinking of buying it—

DENNY Is it of natives with enormous genitals?

JOHN . . . No.

DENNY Look at you, knowing Jessie Brewster. Aren't you the Man About Town?

JOHN Mm.

DENNY Or should I say, Man About *Brown*?

JOHN God, you're disgusting!

DENNY I'm just in a good *mood*!

JOHN Listen, I haven't promised you anything.

DENNY But you will.

JOHN . . . I need a day to think on it.

DENNY I'll give you ten minutes.

JOHN You have to understand I'm implacable.

DENNY *(giggles)*

JOHN Denis.

DENNY I'll get Rose—wait till you meet her—empires
topple—you'll be a breeze!

(GIDGER enters.)

GIDGER The machine is SPEWING paper, and Miss Jessie
Brewster, the tawny nightingale, is seated patiently on a
leather chair, WAITing.

JOHN Yes yes yes—

DENNY I'll go—

What's *on* the paper?

(GIDGER looks at DENNY, turns to JOHN.)

GIDGER Is Mr. McCleary adDRESsing me?

JOHN Yes, I believe he is, Gidger.

GIDGER Is that perMITted?

JOHN Yes, I believe it is, Gidger.

GIDGER *(huffs; then)* Writing of some sort.

JOHN Is it English writing?

DENNY Print or cursive?

JOHN Calligraphy? Rune?

GIDGER . . . I haven't investigated.

DENNY Why not?

GIDGER I'm a little DUTCH boy, I'm STEMming a FLOOD!

JOHN . . . Send in Miss Brewster, will you, Gidger?

GIDGER . . . Well, why not?

(He exits.)

DENNY I'll be right back.

JOHN Oh . . . all right.

DENNY You'll love her, Pace. You'll love us both. It will in*spire* you.

(DENNY *exits.*)

(*A moment.* JESSIE *enters, followed by* GIDGER.)

GIDGER Miss Jessie Brewster, raven-skinned SONGstress.

(*A few sheets of paper come flying through the door.*)

JOHN Miss Brewster.

JESSIE Mr. John Pace Seavering?

JOHN Have a seat, won't you?

JESSIE Yes, thank you.

JOHN . . . GIDGER?

GIDGER (*off stage*) YES?

JOHN HAS MR. McCLEARY GONE YET?

GIDGER (*off stage*) YES!

JOHN THANK YOU!

(*to* JESSIE)

Well . . .

(*then*)

GIDGER?!

GIDGER (*off stage*) YES?

JOHN DO YOU WANT TO TAKE A LITTLE BREAK?

(GIDGER *appears in the doorway, dripping pages.*)

GIDGER Maybe later.

(*He returns to the anteroom.*)

JOHN (*sits*) Well. I've read your book with great interest.

JESSIE I was hoping you had.

JOHN Great interest indeed.

JESSIE And what did you think of it?

JOHN I was mightily impressed.

JESSIE I'm glad.

JOHN And really, you swear it, you worked without a ghost?

JESSIE Every word is my own.

JOHN That's very rare with this kind of thing, you know: very rare.

JESSIE I didn't know.

JOHN Oh, yes.

JESSIE I didn't know.

JOHN The thing about it is, it's so very, very articulate.

JESSIE *(with a slight grimace)* Mmm . . .

JOHN *(quickly)* By which I mean, other performers, when they write their books—when, rather, their books are written for them—tend to bloviate—

JESSIE They . . . ?

JOHN Gas on and on, I mean. Lace and flowers, the real purple. But your writing's quite wonderfully pure.

JESSIE That's because I tell the truth. And truth always purifies a prose style, don't you agree, Mr. Seavering?

JOHN Please call me John.

JESSIE John. And you must call me Jessie.

JOHN . . . Jessie.

　　Well, I don't know if I do agree—

JESSIE You should consider doing so, because I'm right.

　　I see a style all frills and furbelows, I know I am being lied to. Something is being concealed.

　　But give me a march of simple declarative sentences and no lie is possible—there's nowhere to hide.

Don't you show me a *clause* unless the truth is complicated. And the truth hardly ever *is*.

JOHN —Shakespeare—

JESSIE —was a terrible liar.

JOHN He *was*?

JESSIE He couldn't help it.

He lived in a time of courtiers. Lying was the world, what made it move.

He was no exception.

JOHN Most would say he *was* the exception.

JESSIE There are no exceptions to the Times.

JOHN You're a very grand thinker.

JESSIE I'm a very plain thinker. Or else how would I know what I know?

(GIDGER *enters with a stack of pages.*)

GIDGER There has been a TEMporary cesSAtion of machine activity.

JOHN What's all this?

GIDGER From the machine.

JOHN From the ma*chine*?

GIDGER FROM the machine.

JOHN My God.

GIDGER What shall I do with it?

JOHN Oh, put it down somewhere.

GIDGER Anywhere?

JOHN Yes, anywhere.

GIDGER Oh, but no—I would HATE to send this room into disarRAY. I would never forgive myself if I created disorder in your SANCtum messORum.

JOHN That's fine, Gidger.

(GIDGER *gives* JOHN *a look, opens his arms, and lets the pages fall in a pile at his feet.*)

GIDGER I'll be taking a break now.

JOHN Very good.

(GIDGER *starts out, stops.*)

GIDGER *(suddenly)* A STRANGE MACHINE HAS ARRIVED AT YOUR OFFICE UNANNOUNCED! IT HAS SECRET GEARS THAT GRIND, HIDDEN COGS THAT TURN, A CRUDE MECHANICAL WILL, AREN'T YOU EVEN *INTERESTED*?!?!?!?!

JOHN *(mildly)* Whatever it is, I'm sure I can handle it.

(GIDGER, *with his arms outstretched to* JOHN, *looks imploringly at* JESSIE, *as if to say, "Help me with this man." He looks back and forth between the two of them. He might cry but doesn't.*)

GIDGER . . . Don't you ever—don't you EVen—?

JOHN Quite all right, Gidger.

(*Beat.*)

GIDGER Is Gidger my first name or my—

JOHN Why not take that break now?

GIDGER WHY WON'T YOU ACKNOWLEDGE ME?

JESSIE What poets do you like?

(*Beat.*)

GIDGER Are you speaking to ME?

JESSIE Yes. And I wonder: what poets do you like?

GIDGER I favor the SPRUNG rhythms of Gerard MANley Hopkins.

JESSIE Ah yes, Hopkins.

GIDGER Reading him is like walking barefoot on a NEW England beach. You're CONstantly being pricked by unexPECted stones.

(Beat.)

  I'm taking that little break now.

(He exits.)

(JESSIE and JOHN sit silently, listening to him go. The door slams in the anteroom.)

(A door slams more distantly.)

(A moment.)

(They look at each other.)

(JOHN gets up from his desk, crosses to her.)

(He kneels before her chair, puts his head in her lap.)

(He burrows his head in her lap.)

(She places her hands on the sides of his head, draws him up. He kisses up her body.)

(He props himself aslant the chair, holding its arms, and kisses her on the mouth.)

(He leans in to her, kisses her ear.)

(He whispers in her ear. She laughs.)

(She whispers in his ear. He looks shocked—mock shocked.)

(He draws in to her again. She stops him.)

JESSIE Did you mean all that?

JOHN All what?

JESSIE All that you said . . . all that you said for the benefit of that man, that Gadget-man? For the overhearing? Did you mean all that?

JOHN Yes.

JESSIE . . . Huh.

(He goes for her lap again.)

      Easy—easy—easy—

JOHN Gidger will be back in—

JESSIE You young boys—always rushing—

JOHN I'm not a boy—I'm not young—

JESSIE You young white boys—

JOHN I'm colored!

JESSIE Oh really?

JOHN Yes.

JESSIE I don't think so.

JOHN When I'm with you, I am.

JESSIE Oh, you can do that?

JOHN Yes I can.

JESSIE Mercy!

(He laughs.)

JOHN When you say that, you sound like an Englishwoman.

JESSIE Do I?

JOHN "Mercy." "Glory be."

JESSIE Do I? . . . Sho nuf?

JOHN Sho nuf!

      You sound like Queen Victoria when you say that.

      After you get done saying "sho nuf," I have the feeling
someone's been made a knight.

(He starts to nuzzle her.)

JESSIE Retreat a moment, will you?

JOHN No.

JESSIE Well, as a matter of fact . . . *yes.*

(He looks at her, stands, moves away.)

JOHN . . . You're not angry with me, are you?

JESSIE No.

I just want to talk for a bit.

JOHN . . . All right . . . Why?

JESSIE Because we don't much.

JOHN But that's a good thing.

(He smiles.)

We have better things to do . . .

(He kisses her.)

It's good just us, isn't it?

JESSIE It's the only way possible . . .

JOHN People would wreck us . . .

JESSIE Oh yes . . .

JOHN *(with some glee)* They'd be appalled . . .

JESSIE What my people would make of you!

(This throws him.)

JOHN Of *me*?

JESSIE Oh yes.

JOHN No, that's not . . .

No one is ever appalled by me . . .

JESSIE Is that right?

JOHN Yes.

JESSIE And why is that?

JOHN . . .

I don't know.

. . .

I'm what's wanted.

JESSIE *(smiles)* . . . You know so little.

JOHN Teach me the rest.

JESSIE I try, I try.

JOHN Teach me everything. You can—you know everything—you've been all the places they don't let me go—

JESSIE Is it because I'm colored that you love me, or because I'm old?

JOHN Both.

JESSIE If you think a minute, you'll see that's not the right answer.

JOHN I love your book!

JESSIE Oh, it's my *book* you love, not me at all.

JOHN I can't separate the two—I met you at the same time.

JESSIE . . . Come here.

(He approaches.)

(He kneels before her. She offers her wrist.)

(He inhales her fragrance, intoxicated by it.)

(She withdraws her wrist.)

JESSIE That's not the book.

JOHN Oh but it is!

Because when I smell you, do you know what I think of?

Sharecroppers!

JESSIE Dis*gust*ing idea!

JOHN I think of those dinners you had as a child, those dinners you describe in the book: salt pork and a handful of rice—

JESSIE *(fond, amused)* You.

JOHN I think of the distance you've come.

The leap you've made.

The wonder of it.

And how straight you've been through all of it—how you never betrayed yourself, never lied, when why wouldn't you? Given what you've known.

How heroic that is—*you* are.

Everyone around you—succumbing to—narcotics— and despair—plain despair!—but not you. Not you.

And you're with me now—in this tower above a canyon—with the traffic noises all muffled below—and you're famous—and a queen—an Ethiopian—a female— potentate!—grand and tall and smelling marvelously like a department store.

That's the book *and* you.

You *are* each other.

JESSIE There's no helping it, I suppose . . .

JOHN Why should there be? Why should there be?

JESSIE *(private, wistful)* Don't know.

. . . Will you publish it?

JOHN Part of me screams out no, I don't want to publish it—I want to *private* it. I want to secret it beneath my pillow and have it for my dreams.

JESSIE That does *me* no good.

JOHN It's your life, your book is, and that's mine now—it belongs to me—not to anyone who's come before or anyone who's coming later—

JESSIE *(softly)* Actually, it's mine—

JOHN *(slightly overlaps)* Oh God, Jessie—what you are to me!

JESSIE Well, I like you fine, too—

JOHN Everything in my life has always been so—sharp-angled—and obvious—and safe—

JESSIE Oh, safe—

JOHN I've been longing for something clandestine—

JESSIE Clandestine—

JOHN —and here we are—this secret thing—this great, secret thing—and I am so OBSCENELY HAPPY!

(And to show it, he makes a sort of leap, but without letting his feet leave the ground. This upsets his balance, and he falls sideways to the floor.)

(She looks at him, indulgent, amused. He rights himself, sitting, not yet moving to stand.)

JESSIE You young men—

JOHN I tell you, I'm not young—

JESSIE The young men of your generation—who were in the war—

JOHN I'm old—I'm historical—I'm Moses—!

JESSIE —you have made sadness famous.

Yet as a group—I would say you are the most enthusiastic mob I've ever met—

Do you hear me, John?

JOHN I— What?

JESSIE I was questioning the gap between your reputation and your behavior.

JOHN . . . I'm sorry, I wasn't listening, Jessie, I was spinning on an ellipse.

JESSIE I was asking: why are you wrecked men all so damned
    happy? Or is that too much to answer?

JOHN No, I don't think it is.

JESSIE Then tell me.

JOHN I think it's because the century's still so young . . . and
    all the worst things have already happened in it.

JESSIE . . . *Have* they already happened?

JOHN Oh yes, of course.

    Nothing could be worse than the war.

(Beat.)

    And those who've come back . . .

    Some are full of damage, and you see them on the
    streets like—"memento mori!"—and it always makes you
    stumble.

    But then you remember you've survived.

    You've lost your youth, but you've survived.

    And losing your youth, which feels at first like the loss
    of everything, only means that the world isn't the way
    you thought it was.

    But it is some other way.

    And *wantable*.

    So we've started to want it again.

    And it's all hectic inside us—because we never thought
    it would happen, the wanting, never again, but it's there,
    and it's better than any happiness we knew before, when
    life was innocent and uninteresting, and we're all fired up
    by it—and there's always this certainty—under
    everything—under all the uncertainty—that we've been
    through the worst. That it can never be that bad again.

. . .

So if we're . . . lost and . . . ecstatic . . . it's because we
have lost so much . . . and have everything to gain . . .
and *will* gain it.

And those who aren't dead are young.
(She crosses to him, kisses him tenderly.)

Jess . . . ?

I feel so *sure* about things—

JESSIE About what things?

JOHN I don't know. That's the odd part.

I haven't a clue what will *happen* . . . but I know it will
be *right* . . .

JESSIE Oh you do?

JOHN Somehow I do . . .

You know I have no talent of my own—

JESSIE That's not—

JOHN No, it's true, it's completely true. I have no creative
talent of any kind . . .

But I have a sense of who does . . . and this little bit of
money . . . and I know—I *know* that it's all going to lead
somewhere . . . important.

I have power.

I have . . . a sort of mission.

I have . . . this amazing sense of destiny . . . I can't see
it, I can't figure what it will look like . . . but I know it's
there for me.

Is that pompous?

JESSIE *("pompous" doesn't begin . . .)* Oh my *God*—!

JOHN *(a little shy)* Well, I can't help it, it's true . . .

JESSIE Are you publishing my book?

(JOHN *pulls away.*)

JOHN Must you *know*? Must you know right *away*?

JESSIE Yes.

JOHN Why?

JESSIE Because, unlike the people you fought the war with, I am neither dead nor young—

JOHN I need—

JESSIE And I haven't as much century to go as you do—

JOHN Just—

JESSIE And I want to fix myself in people's minds.

JOHN People know you. You're famous—

JESSIE Yes. To the two hundred people who go where I am—

JOHN That's more than most get—

JESSIE It's not enough—

JOHN It should be.

JESSIE Not for *me*.

JOHN If you would just wait—

JESSIE I have *been* waiting. I've waited and waited. I no longer know the reason for the delay.

JOHN I only ask you to be a little *patient*.

(*Beat. She looks at him.*)

JESSIE Oh, John, that is no kind of word to be using with me. Do you know how long I have been . . . *pat*ient?

JOHN . . .

I'm sorry, Jess.

JESSIE Sorry!

Oh, is that what you are? Sorry?

JOHN Jess—

JESSIE You sit here . . . in this . . . haphazard room that looks like *weather's* happened to it—without an inkling of the future—or an instinct to your name—except you know— you *know*—that whatever you do, it will turn out all right.

But I'm nearly fourteen years older than you, and by myself I can only go so far and *that is not as far as I mean to go.*

So I need you.

I need *you*, John.

Your help.

The help of a baby—

JOHN I'm not a baby—

JESSIE Oh God, you even *smell* new!

JOHN Jessie—

JESSIE It's not enough to be famous to a few dozen drunks in evening clothes who condescend to worship me.

I want my life known. I want to publish my life.

I want to nail it into people's heads.

JOHN Jesus, Jessie—that's a pretty gruesome way to put it.

JESSIE Don't take that tone. Don't pretend you don't want to be shocked by me.

JOHN . . . The thing is, you see . . . I only have very limited resources—I can only publish *one* book—

JESSIE Lucky for you, I've only written one book.

JOHN *You* have, yes.

(Beat. She hears his inflection, her mind goes to work.)

JESSIE Who was that young man?

JOHN . . . The—

JESSIE Who was here with you when I arrived.

JOHN Oh, Denny! That's Denis McCleary. He's just a friend
from school.

JESSIE Oh, I see, just a friend from school.

    . . .

    Are you fucking him?

JOHN . . . GOD!

    Of course not—GOD! What kind of—

JESSIE Well, you *are* fucking me—

JOHN Which should have answered your question—

JESSIE *(dismissive laugh)* Oh, John—

JOHN Sometimes you go too far, you know.

JESSIE Has he written a book?

JOHN . . . No, I wouldn't say so.

JESSIE Because every word he writes will be a lie.

JOHN You don't even know him.

JESSIE You don't have to make the acquaintance of that sort
of person to know him.

JOHN He's all right . . .

JESSIE That's a weak thing to say.

JOHN Don't call me that—

JESSIE Tell me, John: are you really a publisher?

JOHN I am . . . I mean to be a publisher.

JESSIE Then *publ*ish something.

JOHN . . . It's so hard . . . to decide.

    It's so hard to *act*—

JESSIE But the future is in your pocket—

JOHN And I don't want to mess that up!

  I need a crystal ball . . . if only I could *know*—

JESSIE But you can't. You can't know how anything will turn out . . . all you can do is what's right.

JOHN And how do I know what *that* is?

JESSIE *I* am what's right.

  Your college friends are all liars. They're liars, charlatans, no-talents, and drunks—they will have no trouble achieving publication.

  I need YOU.

JOHN . . . Give me—

JESSIE There is no *time*! There is no such thing as time.

JOHN —a day—

JESSIE *(on "day")* Is it all right to fuck a nigger but you don't want to be a nigger press? Is that—?

JOHN Jesus! You *know* that isn't—

JESSIE *(on "know")* Do you want to be my lover, John?

JOHN . . . I *am* your lover—

JESSIE *(on "lover")* Do you wish to remain so?

JOHN Is that contingent on—

JESSIE No, of course not.

  Except that with everything you do or fail to do, you will reveal yourself to me.

  And everything I learn, I will assess.

  And when I know what manner of man you are, I will decide if you suit me.

JOHN . . . You can't run out on me, Jess; I can't . . . do without you, you know.

JESSIE And I don't want to.

I like most things about you.

I like talking with you . . . and sleeping with you . . .

and cradling your head . . .

My baby boy . . . my *child* . . . !

I even like being your secret . . . and having you for mine.

But I won't be your lie—

JOHN You're not—

JESSIE Oh yes—the little thing you brag to yourself about.

The tiny violence that violates nothing.

JOHN I won't make a promise that I can't—

JESSIE Everything you *do* is a promise, John.

"Good morning" is a promise when you say it.

JOHN Give me just—

JESSIE Are we going to the theater tonight?

JOHN *(startled by the subject shift)* Yes! I found the tickets!

JESSIE Shall we meet for drinks before?

JOHN Yes.

JESSIE I'll stop by here at about seven.

JOHN That will be . . . lovely . . .

JESSIE And you'll tell me what you've decided.

(The doors to the anteroom fly open, and we hear the thunderous tick-tick-tick of the new machine. GIDGER, DENNY, *and* ROSAMUND PLINTH *enter, almost abreast, amidst a storm of flying pages that threatens to inundate the room.)*

GIDGER I COULDN'T STOP THEM—

DENNY *(overlaps)* IT'S LIKE TICKER TAPE—

ROSAMUND *(overlaps)* I said to Denny: What a marvelous greeting from a publishing house—

GIDGER *(overlaps)* DO YOU *SEE*? DO YOU *SEE* WHAT'S
  GOING ON?

JOHN *(overlaps)* GIDGER! STOP THOSE PAPERS
  FLYING—

DENNY *(overlaps)* ISN'T THIS THE MOST PHENOMENAL
  STORM? WHEE!

(He and ROSAMUND *start spinning around like happy
children as* GIDGER *fights to close the doors against the
onslaught.)*

ROSAMUND *(overlaps)* It reminds me of cotillion one time
  when—

JOHN *(overlaps)* CALL SOMEBODY, WOULD YOU! A
  PLUMBER OR SOMETHING!

ROSAMUND *(overlaps)*—or was it a May Day fling?—there
  were streamers everywhere and oh how we laughed!

DENNY *(overlaps)* YOU'RE A GENIUS, JOHNNY! A G.D.
  GENIUS!

GIDGER *(overlaps)* TEN MINUTES TO GET *COFFEE* AND—

ROSAMUND *(overlaps)* This is quite innovative, I hope there
  are people from the press here to cover it . . .

*(*GIDGER *has successfully closed the doors, and
ROSAMUND's last phrases are spoken in the clear.)*
*(And we get to hear her voice, which is the silken,
musical voice of a rich American girl that belongs to no
region and stops exactly as short of self-parody as those
girls do. She is beautiful and more charming than
everyone you've ever met.)*
(A pause as everyone recovers and realizes ROSAMUND
is there.)

ROSAMUND I say: I hope someone here is a member of the press, because this sort of thing should be noticed . . .

(Pause.)

*(*ROSAMUND *extends her hand to* JOHN.*)*

　　Let me do the honors: I'm Rosamund Plinth—

DENNY *(catching himself, overlaps)* This is Rosamund Plinth?

ROSAMUND *(tilts her head, scrutinizes his face)* Have we *met* before?

JOHN No, I'm sure not.

DENNY This is Rosamund Plinth—

JOHN I'm John Seavering—

ROSAMUND *(overlaps, to* DENNY*)* Yes, he knows I'm Rosamund Plinth, I said so—

DENNY *(overlaps)* This is John Pace Seavering—

ROSAMUND So good to meet you—

(She turns to JESSIE, *extends hand.)*

　　I'm Rosamund Plinth—

JOHN *(overlaps)* This is Jessie Brewster—

JESSIE *(overlaps)* I'm Jessie Brewster—

ROSAMUND So good to meet you.

(Tilts head, scrutinizes JESSIE'*s face.)*

　　Have we *met* before?

JESSIE Absolutely not.

DENNY She's the colored singer—

ROSAMUND *(overlaps)* Oh, you're the singer!

JOHN Yes. Miss Brewster is a very fine—

ROSAMUND I saw you perform just last week.

JESSIE I didn't perform last week.

ROSAMUND I enjoyed it very much.

JESSIE I'm so glad.

ROSAMUND You make that *noise*, don't you, that very distinctive *noise*. I've never heard it anywhere else, except once from this woman in Fez, that sort of trill. Where the top note flutters high high high to heaven and the bottom note dives down down down to hell and the whole effect is uncanny and unsettling but altogether riveting. Yes, you're a genius.

(Pause.)

Well.

I hope we haven't inter*rup*ted a *con*clave of some sort.

JESSIE I was just leaving—

ROSAMUND *(overlaps)* It's just Denny and I got so excited about your promise to publish his *book*, Mr. Seavering—

(JESSIE shoots JOHN a look.)

JOHN I . . .

(Pause.)

ROSAMUND We couldn't help ourselves.

(Pause.)

JOHN Ah.

(Beat.)

DENNY I told you not to mention it—

ROSAMUND *(overlaps)* Oh, I hope I haven't spoken out of turn—

JESSIE *(overlaps)* Of course not, but I must be off, there are some people . . .

(Pause.)

GIDGER DOESN'T ANYONE CARE THAT SOMETHING

PHENOMENOLOGICAL IS HAPPENING IN THE *VERY*
NEXT *ROOM?*

(Pause.)

JESSIE So, John, I'll come by at seven?

JOHN Yes: seven.

DENNY With the painting?

(JOHN and JESSIE look at him, then at each other.)

JESSIE No, it's too large to carry.

(She opens the door; just a flurry of pages. She exits,
followed by GIDGER.)

DENNY Do you have cigarettes?

JOHN Yes.

DENNY I'll get some!

(He exits.)

(JOHN and ROSAMUND are alone.)

ROSAMUND Is he subtle, would you call him? Would you call
him subtle?

JOHN He seemed to want to leave us alone . . . for some
reason.

ROSAMUND Yes.

I'm to seduce you.

JOHN !

ROSAMUND Oh, I don't mean with *sex*—well, yes, I *do* mean
with sex—I *don't* mean with intercourse—

Are you sure we haven't met each other?

JOHN Yes. Quite sure.

(A moment.)

Still . . .

ROSAMUND Yes, what is it?

RICHARD GREENBERG

JOHN I'm . . . not . . .

ROSAMUND Perhaps it's that I've met so many of you and you've met so many of me that it's as *if* we've met each other . . .

JOHN . . . Why don't you sit?

ROSAMUND Why don't I indeed?

JOHN Would you like to smoke?

ROSAMUND Yes. I would.

(He gets cigarettes, lights them. They smoke.)

JOHN What purpose does he suppose it would serve, your "seducing" me?

ROSAMUND Oh, Denny . . .

JOHN What does that mean: "Oh, Denny"? . . .

ROSAMUND . . . I think he must have had a great many promises broken to him in his life, don't you? I think when you grow up a certain way . . . when you don't gain admittance to certain rooms . . . or do, but too late, and with all the wrong feelings about them . . . there must always be something a bit *off* in your rhythm, something that makes you never at ease.

(Beat.)

Possibly that's all to the good . . .

JOHN Do you feel at ease now?

ROSAMUND Yes! Ever so.

JOHN But you— *(stops himself)*

ROSAMUND Oh, say it, I don't mind—

JOHN . . . You were brought up in a slaughterhouse.

ROSAMUND I was brought up in a big square mansion . . .

JOHN . . . where big square things happened?

ROSAMUND All the time.

JOHN On a daily basis.

ROSAMUND Yes: on a daily basis.

(Beat.)

I do like the looks of this room.

JOHN We're having a bit of a—

ROSAMUND Yes—I can *see* that—

JOHN Ma*chine* uproar—

ROSAMUND That's what I like—

JOHN I expect we'll have it in order soon—

ROSAMUND I expect you will.

(They look at each other.)

We're *mar*velously comfortable with each other, aren't we?

JOHN Yes—

ROSAMUND Your breathing even changes around me, doesn't it?

Oh, I don't mean because I'm so be*witch*ing—I don't think I'm be*witch*ing—I don't mean it gets all fast and huffy. I mean the opposite. I mean you relax.

(Beat.)

Because even though I was reared in a slaughterhouse and you in an Episcopal bell tower, we've . . . come together.

(Beat.)

So that you can say things to me that would surprise some of the other people you know who think, I think, that you're a mild and cautious young man.

(Beat.)

    Isn't that what they think?

    That you're a mild and cautious young man?

(Beat.)

    But to me you can say things like "you were brought up in a slaughterhouse," and I'll know the exact limit of your daring and that I'm being flirted with, not insulted. And that the flirtation will only go so far and really isn't flirty at all but only a sort of code for "hello."

(Beat.)

    This is a very pleasant little rest for me—I've been spending so much time with Denny's friends—oh! they must be your friends, too—and they're not at all restful. They arrive in clumps and leave in tatters.

JOHN And how do you find them?

ROSAMUND Absolutely eighty proof!

(Beat.)

    Denny thinks you're a mild and cautious young man. They all do, the clump, the tattered clump . . .

    They mock you a bit.

JOHN Do they?

ROSAMUND Oh, adoringly . . .

    Oh, of course you know that, they do it to your face, I'm sure . . .

    It's not worse than what they say to your face, I'm sure . . . The sad thing, of course, is that they feel tenderly towards you . . . because they're so coarse and wicked and you're so sweet and unsuspecting . . .

Isn't that sad?

When we both know . . .

Oh, but why go into that?

(Beat.)

Listen, we're so terribly excited you're publishing this book.

JOHN . . . Denny . . . may not completely understand what I told him.

(Hesitation.)

ROSAMUND *(frozen smile)* What are you saying?

(Beat.)

JOHN I told him only . . . that I was con*si*dering publishing his—

ROSAMUND Do you understand what's riding on this?

JOHN Yes. For me, too—

ROSAMUND Everything is riding on this—

JOHN Exactly—

ROSAMUND You can't go around withdrawing your promises—

JOHN I've made no—

ROSAMUND —as it suits you—

JOHN —-promises of any kind—

ROSAMUND You are publishing his book! There! That's all there is to it!

(She throws her cigarette down and mashes it into the floor with her foot.)

JOHN . . . You've mashed your cigarette into my floor!

ROSAMUND Well, it's not as if it makes anything *worse*.

(He looks at her, flabbergasted.)

Oh, what have I done?

(She drops to the floor and collects the ashes.)

JOHN No . . . don't.

(He joins her there.)

ROSAMUND I shouldn't have—

JOHN That's all right—

ROSAMUND I'm so . . . *so* . . .

(She closes her eyes in frustration, planting her fist in her hand.)

JOHN Rosamund . . . ?

(She smiles at him reassuringly and offers him her hand. He helps her up. She straightens herself and crosses to the window.)

Can I . . . do something . . . ?

ROSAMUND Oh no . . . no need . . .

(Beat. She turns to him.)

Does life ever become transparent for you?

JOHN Transparent?

ROSAMUND Do you ever have presentiments? Are you ever certain what will happen?

JOHN No. Never.

ROSAMUND Well, I am sometimes.

I am now.

Denny and I—we're the only happiness that will ever be possible to each other.

JOHN . . . Then *take* each other.

ROSAMUND It's not so easy. There's my father . . .

Oh, don't make a mistake about him—he's a very kind man.

And a very prudent one.

All he asks is some evidence that *something* will
become of Denny. And then he'll give us his blessing.

JOHN And if there is no evidence, right away . . . and you
marry anyway?

ROSAMUND He'll disinherit me.

JOHN Then live poor.

ROSAMUND *(not an attack; wistful)* Oh John . . .

JOHN If you love him—

ROSAMUND Love doesn't necessarily abolish intelligence.
Denny is a Catholic.

JOHN *Lapsed* Catholic.

ROSAMUND His faith has lapsed, his psyche remains devout.
He's a great self-tormenter. If I were to give up
everything, the burden would be intolerable—it would
destroy us.
And there's another man . . . waiting in the wings . . .
who will not, not ever, no never, be poor. If things didn't
turn out for us, the specter of—

JOHN Yes, I know about him.

ROSAMUND Oh, you do.

JOHN This man Armitage.

ROSAMUND Yes. This man Armitage.

JOHN . . . And what kind of life would you have with him?

ROSAMUND . . . A fine life.

JOHN Do you love him?

ROSAMUND . . . I used to think so.

JOHN But since Denny came along . . .

ROSAMUND . . . the concept has been redefined.

JOHN And your feelings for Armitage?

ROSAMUND . . . have not diminished.

(Beat.)

It's just they don't compare.

(Beat.)

Won't you publish this book?

JOHN . . . All I know is . . . maybe.

ROSAMUND . . . Ah.

. . .

Tell me . . . do you think it's a good book?

JOHN Have you read it?

ROSAMUND Pieces.

JOHN That's all you— It's *in* pieces.

What do you think?

ROSAMUND I don't know what to think.

The grammar's atrocious. You wonder how he got through Princeton—

JOHN He didn't—

ROSAMUND Those three years . . . with grammar like that.

And most of the ideas are sophomoric—

JOHN Most of it was written sophomore year—

ROSAMUND And yet . . .

JOHN . . . Yes.

ROSAMUND It's something I've never seen before.

JOHN There's no one like Denny.

ROSAMUND *You're* in love with him, too.

(JOHN looks startled. ROSAMUND laughs her beguiling laugh.)

JOHN *(to himself)* Well, it's all *right*, it's just a *laugh*, it's not great.

ROSAMUND Pardon?

(She looks at him vulnerably, appealingly, and it touches him.)

JOHN Why don't you wait? Why don't you wait and see how things pan out? Why must you run into the arms of another man?

ROSAMUND I'm not young . . . something has to be done with me.

JOHN Denny says you paint . . . and dance . . . and . . . so forth . . . Why not strike out on your own? Why not be an artist yourself?

ROSAMUND *(and this single syllable contains so much regret)* Oh . . .

(Pause.)

JOHN I see.

(GIDGER rushes in; paper swirls.)

GIDGER These PAges are belonging together and there's SOMEthing very strange about it—

JOHN Gidger, I'm talking to Miss Plinth—

GIDGER *(swirling out)* All right, but this is something you should KNOW about—

(Meanwhile, ROSAMUND has wandered to the window, where she looks statuesque and stricken.)

JOHN Oh, don't look like that . . . don't look like that . . .

Like La Señorita Dolorosa . . .

This portrait—this photograph of sadness—

I don't want you looking like that . . .

ROSAMUND It's just for the moment.

JOHN Your father is a wicked man.

ROSAMUND He's a wise—an in*tel*ligent man—

JOHN Those are euphemisms—

ROSAMUND There's nothing treacherous about foresight, John . . . It doesn't lessen the force of love . . . or taint its quality. All anyone is thinking of is happiness . . .

JOHN Sometimes it's better to take a leap in the dark.

ROSAMUND But when there's no darkness available to you?

JOHN Yes, I forgot, you have the gift of prophecy.

ROSAMUND I never said it was a gift . . .

(GIDGER enters.)

GIDGER JOHN Pace SEAVERING!

JOHN I'm in the middle of something, Gidger—

GIDGER Yes, this VALE of tears we call LIFE, HOWever—

ROSAMUND *(gathering her things to go)* I am staying at the Plaza—

GIDGER There's something I must tell you—

JOHN You have an apartment on Fifth Avenue—

GIDGER These PAges—

ROSAMUND Yes, but sometimes I like to pretend I'm a tourist, and I take a room in the Plaza—

GIDGER JOHN!

JOHN Hush, Gidger!

ROSAMUND I can do things in rooms in the Plaza that I can't do in rooms I own—

GIDGER BUT—

ROSAMUND You *have* persuaded me of one thing in our little talk, John—

JOHN What is that?

(The machine starts making loud ticking noises.)

GIDGER *(flurrying off)* O-O-O-O-O-H-H!!!

ROSAMUND That life for me without Denny is impossible—

JOHN That's not what I—

ROSAMUND I'm meant to return to Chicago tomorrow—if I return, there's meant to be a party for me—to announce my engagement to Mr. Armitage—

GIDGER *(offstage)* OH MY GOD!

ROSAMUND But I shall not announce my engagement to Mr. Armitage—

GIDGER *(offstage)* OH! MY! GOD!

ROSAMUND Because if you haven't agreed to publish Denny's book by this evening, I'm going to toss myself out the fourteenth-floor window of my room at the Plaza Hotel—

JOHN Rosamund!

ROSAMUND Good day, Mr. Seavering.

(She exits. After a startled second, JOHN *lunges after her.)*

JOHN ROSAMUND!

*(*GIDGER *enters, grabs* JOHN.*)*

GIDGER John—!

(A door slams.)

JOHN Let me go, Gidger—

GIDGER LIS-ten to ME!—

(Another door slams.)

JOHN ROSAMUND!

GIDGER I've been reading these *pages*—these pages are from

authentic BOOKS—these books come from the END of
the century—

JOHN So? So?

GIDGER John! *This* century—!

(An instant. JOHN *turns sharply to* GIDGER.*)*
(Fast curtain.)

(End Act One.)

ACT TWO

GIDGER *and* JOHN *sit in chairs reading.*

GIDGER *wears a bookkeeper's eyeshade.* JOHN's *vest is undone and his tie loosened.*

Pages are stacked about them in a semblance of order.

Lamps are on. It is late afternoon. They have been reading for hours and hours.

There is a sense of gravity about things.

Silent reading for quite some time.

GIDGER What's World War *One*?

JOHN . . . Our recent conflagration.

GIDGER Oh.

(He returns to reading, looks up.)

You're sure of that?

JOHN Yes.

GIDGER I see.

(He returns to reading, looks up.)

Why "One"?

*(*JOHN *looks at him.)*

Oh. I see.

(He goes back to reading, looks up.)

Then it stops being called the "Great War"?

JOHN Yes.

*(*GIDGER *goes back to reading, looks up.)*

GIDGER . . . It gets demoted?

JOHN No. I wouldn't say demoted . . .

Added to.

(Beat.)

Half of a *brace*.

GIDGER Ah.

. . .

What are the causes—

JOHN Complicated, complicated— .

GIDGER Oh.

. . .

Shall we exchange pages?

JOHN Not yet.

GIDGER All right.

(Beat. They read.)

GIDGER —Why did this machine come to us?

JOHN I don't know.

GIDGER . . . Was it a prank?

JOHN I thought so at first.

I thought my father sent it to undo me.

GIDGER Your father?

JOHN Yes.

GIDGER Why would your father want to undo you?

JOHN Because I'm defying him.

Because I'm taking only so much of his money and no more, and using it to smash everything he believes in.

Because he wants to control me and I won't let him.

Because we're natural enemies.

GIDGER Oh.

(Beat.)

But isn't it our *mothers* we hate?

JOHN Only for a few more years.

GIDGER And then it's our fathers?

JOHN Yes, it seems so.

GIDGER What do you know?

JOHN I—yes.

GIDGER Huh!

Fickle.

(Beat.)

I wish it hadn't come.

JOHN Yes.

GIDGER I wish it had never come here.

JOHN Yes.

GIDGER I mean, it's compelling reading, but I'm not enjoying myself.

(JOHN looks up, smiles sadly.)

GIDGER Let's stop.

JOHN All right.

(They stop reading.)

(Pause.)

(They go back to reading.)

GIDGER I know: let's go somewhere, you and I. Let's leave

these pages and go to a bar or somewhere—where we
can drink and spout philosophy and be terribly gay!

(JOHN *laughs.*)

Why are you laughing?

JOHN A word you used.

GIDGER What word?

JOHN "Gay."

GIDGER . . . I'm flummoxed.

JOHN It doesn't mean what you think.

GIDGER I think it does.

JOHN It means something else.

GIDGER When?

JOHN Late-mid-century at the latest.

GIDGER What?

JOHN Homosexual, chiefly male.

(*Beat.*)

GIDGER "Gay" means "homosexual, chiefly male"?

JOHN Yes.

(GIDGER *ponders this.*)

GIDGER . . . What's the connection?

JOHN I don't know the etymology, just the outcome . . .

(*Beat.*)

GIDGER Then what word means gay?

JOHN As far as I can tell, there is none . . .

GIDGER But how can that *be*?

JOHN As far as I can tell, it's no longer needed.

Lacking a word, the quality disappears.

GIDGER Why? WHY? Why?

JOHN It seems, by century's end, the prevailing note is a sort of dark general frivolity for which almost everyone has contempt but that no one does anything to change.

GIDGER But gaiety has nothing to do with frivolity! Gaiety has the utmost existential seriousness!

JOHN Existential?

GIDGER What made me say that?

JOHN I don't know.

GIDGER *(tasting the word)* Ex-is-ten-tial.

I don't know what it means, but it sounds popular.

JOHN . . . Is it . . . Kierkegaard?

GIDGER I don't know.

JOHN I've always meant to read Kierkegaard.

I've read Hegel . . . I've even believed him!

I have such terrible gaps . . .

GIDGER Gaiety gone!

How do they live without it?

JOHN I don't know.

GIDGER To be gay is not to be frivolous.

JOHN I know.

GIDGER To be gay is to be lighthearted in the face of every kind of darkness.

To insist on one's own happiness when God or the forces of chaos rally to oppose it.

To fill a void. To make a void a NICHE.

To understand that the future is at BEST . . . bleakness deferred.

And to go on.

So *those* people no longer exist because . . . *(darkly)* *those* people have co-opted their name.

JOHN "Co-opted"?

GIDGER It means . . . take over, I think.

JOHN Take over?

GIDGER Appropriate.

JOHN Oh.

Co-opted.

(He shivers.)

GIDGER Well.

I don't care what *those* people think: *I* am gay.

Gaygaygay!

There!

(Beat.)

Do you know what those people *do*?

JOHN I've never been sure.

GIDGER Well: imagine a thermometer and then—

JOHN I'd rather not.

(GIDGER looks at him.)

(They return to reading. After a moment, JOHN groans.)

GIDGER What?

JOHN Trippy dies of acute alcohol poisoning—

GIDGER *(barely looking up)* When?

JOHN In twelve years—

GIDGER Hm.

JOHN We only have him twelve more—

GIDGER Well, he was always kind of a creep.

(JOHN looks at GIDGER.)

JOHN *(ambivalent)* . . . Yes.

(They return to reading.)

Oh *no*!

RICHARD GREENBERG

GIDGER *What?*

JOHN Wilson dies in a Times Square hotel room, anonymously, his body isn't discovered for four days. Berringer shoots himself; Albert goes for cigarettes and is never heard from again. Tomlinson dies of alcohol, Kerrigan becomes an opium fiend, Kefauver writes for television— Swedenson dies of alcohol, Derby dies of alcohol, Epper alcohol.

Bundy goes mad. Katz goes mad.

Bartley dies of syphilis, Vance in a car crash.

Imminger drugs.

. . . Everyone I know suffers a tragic fate!

GIDGER *(who has been going intently and rapidly through pages)* And I'm not mentioned anywhere!

JOHN But . . . my intentions are so good . . .

(The phone rings. JOHN goes to it.)

JOHN Yes . . . yes . . . Oh, she hasn't . . . Yes, I see.

Well, this is awfully good of you.

If she does come in, please please have her call me.

(He hangs up.)

The Plaza.

I asked them to call if Rosamund came in.

She didn't but they heard the note of urgency in my voice and called anyway . . . to assure me they were on it.

GIDGER They know how to behave at the Plaza.

JOHN Yes.

GIDGER . . . Does *that* continue, at least?

(JOHN shrugs.)

I suppose we'll find out eventually.

JOHN Gidger?

GIDGER Yes, John?

JOHN Why are you talking like that?

GIDGER U-u-u-h-h like what?

JOHN Why has your voice stopped spiking?

GIDGER Has it?

JOHN Yes.

GIDGER *Has* it?

JOHN Yes.

GIDGER *(effortfully)* My VOICE has STOPPED spiKING . . .

My voice HAS stopped SPI . . .

(He looks to JOHN, *who shakes his head: No, that's not it.)*

Well . . . what's the use of being original if you're going to die in COMPLETE OBSCURITY?

JOHN I just read a conversation I had yesterday.

GIDGER With whom?

JOHN Bartley.

GIDGER Had he died of syphilis yet?

JOHN No.

GIDGER Well, he will.

JOHN It wasn't much of a conversation.

But he transcribed every word.

Why did he take it all down? Why are we all such recordists?

Don't we know that . . . ?

Everyone's taking everything down as if it's historical, as if it's *historic*.

As if it's witty or sums up the Times.

All of us confident, all of us aquiver with self-importance. I've read things I said three weeks ago, and things I said three years ago, and things that were said back to me. And things that were not said quite that way, and things that were said back but not quite so well.

Gidger?

(Beat.)

We all sound alike.

I thought we were each unique.

I held our distinctions in such high regard.

I thought our nuances were essential.

I can't hear them anymore.

When I read them . . . I don't hear them.

We all sound the same.

(Beat.)

We sound like the past.

Even you, Gidger—even back when you seemed the opposite of everything—you were just . . . a different tempo in the same signature—I don't want to think about it.

(He crosses to the window.)

On the street there's a woman standing in front of a shopwindow. Her chin is propped on her finger. She's trying to decide whether to buy a dress.

Across the street from her—she doesn't see this—a man is taking her photograph.

I know what the photograph will look like. All shades of gray and the light bunching behind her, that ghost look.

. . .

This all happened *ages* ago.

Look at us, Gidger—we're *per*iod.

These aren't clothes we're wearing—they're costumes.

(The phone rings. JOHN *grabs it.)*

Yes?

Oh . . . oh, thank you, yes, I'm very grateful to you . . .

Oh, she hasn't . . .

Yes, please, I would so appreciate it.

Yes, thank you very much.

(He hangs up.)

The concierge at Miss Plinth's building . . . she hasn't appeared, but he heard the note of concern in my voice . . . and . . .

. . .

People were so considerate back when we lived.

(A moment. His brow furrows in confusion.)

GIDGER I've found something about you.

JOHN Oh . . . ?

GIDGER In a book about something else . . . Oh, it's nice!

JOHN When is it written?

GIDGER . . . 1959.

JOHN Ah . . .

GIDGER *(reads)* ". . . until his recent retirement represented the beau ideal in American publishing . . ."

JOHN Oh . . .

GIDGER *(scans page for more)* ". . . his example reminds us that the root meaning of 'virtue' is 'manliness' . . ."

You are *well liked* in 1959!

JOHN *(quietly)* Well . . . that's 1959 . . .

GIDGER *Does* she jump?

(JOHN looks bewildered by the question. GIDGER indicates all the manuscript pages.)

JOHN . . . I don't know.

I haven't yet seen that text.

GIDGER Well, it doesn't matter.

JOHN Gidger!

GIDGER I only mean . . . whatever will be . . . will be . . .

(Returns to reading. After a moment, he hums a chorus of "Qué Será, Será" . . . or rather, a chorus of "Qué Será, Será" hums itself through him. He has no idea what it is.)

(He and JOHN look at each other in complete bewilderment.)

(The machine goes tick-tick-tick . . .)

GIDGER I'll get that . . . !

(GIDGER exits.)

(JOHN looks around the room. Sighs.)

(He walks among the towers of texts, this miniature city.)

(JESSIE enters.)

JESSIE What have you read?

(GIDGER enters behind her.)

GIDGER Miss Jessie Brewster, Dusky Darktown Diva—

JESSIE What do you know?

JOHN Thank you very much, Gidger.

JESSIE *Talk* to me—

JOHN Gidger, Miss Brewster and I need to speak.

GIDGER . . . Oh! You mean *alone*?

JOHN Yes.

GIDGER Fine. I'll find something to read.

(He exits.)

JESSIE John, what's—

*(*JOHN *puts his finger to his lips, nodding to where* GIDGER *was. They move away from the door.)*

JESSIE What gets learned?

JOHN I must have sounded insane to you on the phone . . .

JESSIE No.

JOHN How could I not?

JESSIE Anything that causes dread makes sense to me.

. . .

What's found out?

JOHN . . . *We* are.

JESSIE How? By whom?

JOHN Anna Vale Darlington.

JESSIE And *who* is Anna Vale Darlington?

JOHN A writer . . . some sort of writer.

JESSIE How does she find out about us?

JOHN We leave traces.

JESSIE And this book is published?

JOHN Yes.

JESSIE When?

JOHN 1992.

(Pause.)

JESSIE Then we've all died.

JOHN I don't have that volume.

. . .

Of *course* we have. We must have.

Certainly *you.*

. . .

Unless extraordinary things have happened.

Extraordinary things happen!

JESSIE What sort of things have you read?

What "traces" do we leave?

JOHN I only have sections . . . pages come spewing out . . .
we try to order them.

There are letters.

Apparently we save each other's letters.

JESSIE Show me.

(JOHN *hands her the manuscript.*)

JESSIE *(reading)* "My Sheba,

I'm supposed to be working, instead I think of you.
How I love to grab you by your plum-colored arms and
draw you in to me, your breath stirring me with its
redolence of lilacs and the sea, your black but comely
cheek pressed to mine—"

You never wrote this, I never got this from you.

(*He crosses to desk, opens drawer, takes out sheet of
paper, hands it to her. She reads it.*)

JOHN I meant to send it today. I was going to . . . send it . . .

. . . It sounds . . . ex*cru*ciating . . . Is it?

Is it as . . . foolish as I think?

JESSIE *(gently indicating the manuscript)* Here it is.
(indicating the letter)

But somehow not here . . .

JOHN It's the most confounding thing . . . this thing that's

going on . . . I thought I was an intelligent man . . . It
seems I'm wrong—

JESSIE You are an intelligent—

JOHN Not just about that . . . about *everything*.

JESSIE What does this book say?

JOHN Here.

Maybe you can explain it to me.

I can't understand it at all.

This part:

(She comes close. He reads.)

"Her characteristic sound, for which she became
famous, is something that voice teachers call la voce di
strega—the voice of the witch. It's a kind of trill in which
a cultivated head tone alternates rapidly with a raw,
booming, hollow note from the chest. In this bifurcated
sound, Jessie Brewster slyly encoded the fierce and
rending division between her African roots and her
European aspirations . . ."

(He turns to her.)

Is that . . . why you make that . . . ?

JESSIE I just thought it sounded interesting . . .

JOHN *(nods, returns to text)* Here—this is . . . us . . .
(Reads.)

". . . but this was no meeting of innocent souls . . . For
underlying, indeed, pervading, this relationship were
concurrent and overlapping scripts . . ."

*(He looks at her. She shakes her head, not
understanding.)*

". . . of whiteness and negritude . . ."

(He shakes his head. She leans on him.)

". . . maleness and femaleness . . ."

(He nods; that makes sense to him.)

". . . overclass and underclass . . ."

(Unconsciously, she begins to twirl her finger in his hair.)

". . . master and slave . . ."

(They smile, a little shyly, at each other.)

". . . mother and child . . ."

(They look a little abashed.)

". . . all performed within a framework of the self-consciously 'illicit,' inflected on both sides by a fetishizing of the 'primitive,' and marked by strong homosexual role play . . ."

(He looks up.)

It seems to be written in patois.

(He reads again.)

"In this study, I propose not so much a conventional 'biography' as a reading of a hitherto undiscovered relationship between two important figures in the arts in the early part of the century. The approach I take is consonant with my training in anthropology, comparative literature, African-American studies, European history, Indo-European history, cultural history, pop-cultural history, feminist history, queer theory, structuralist theory, post-structuralist theory, modernist theory, postmodern theory, Lacan, Foucault, Derrida, Said, de Saussure—"

(GIDGER enters, brandishing pages.)

GIDGER Oh my God: we are never again eating *red meat*!

(He exits. They go back to the text, skip a page.)

JOHN Chapter One—

JESSIE Don't read it.

JOHN But—

JESSIE What's the point? We know everything that's in it . . . or we will.

JOHN It feels as if I don't know *any* of it . . . it's all so *strange* . . .

I'm on the brink of everything, and it's like an *end*ing.

Everything seems to be spinning, and I can't move . . .

Ever since this started, I've felt sick for some reason . . .

I've felt ashamed . . .

Nothing connects to anything . . .

Could this have been my life?

JESSIE No.

JOHN But . . . all these *words*—

JESSIE Stop reading them.

JOHN How can I stop reading them when they're *there*?

JESSIE Stop caring.

JOHN But I *do* care—terribly.

JESSIE Then act like someone who doesn't.

JOHN You can't do that—you can't make yourself into something you're not.

JESSIE *That* is the only truly stupid thing I've ever heard you say.

(GIDGER enters, sincerely hurt.)

GIDGER . . . Why didn't you tell me?

JOHN Gidger, we—

GIDGER HOW COULD YOU KEEP IT FROM ME?

JOHN What, Gidger, what are you talking about?

GIDGER You two are mis*cege*nating?

(Beat.)

JOHN Where did you—

GIDGER Under my *very* eyes?

JOHN How did you find that out?

GIDGER Did you think I would *judge* you?

Did you really think that *little* of me?

JOHN How did you find that out, Gidger—

GIDGER This is so bogus!

You are really bumming my trip!

You have turned into one dicty ofay, bro—treating me like I'm a *day* player and you're the whole *mini*series.

All day long this machine is buggin', but I'm all-the-way-with-Adlai, I'm doing the right thing.

You *owe* me for that, dude.

Man works for you twenty-four/seven, you've got to give him his *props*!

(And he's flabbergasted by the festival of alien slang he's unleashed.)

What am I *talking* about?

JESSIE Is there another copy—

GIDGER I don't *rec*ognize myself.

JESSIE Is there, Gidger?

GIDGER I don't even exist—I'm just a *con*duit for history!

JESSIE Is there another copy of this book—are they *out*?—

can people get them?—

GIDGER (*looks at the manuscript* JESSIE's *holding*) It's
  another book.

JESSIE . . . Another—

JOHN Another book?

GIDGER . . . Yes.

(JOHN *and* JESSIE *look at each other, apprehensive.*)

JOHN What *is* the other book, Gidger?

(GIDGER *hands him some pages.*)

(JOHN *reads.*)

  "John Pace Seavering: A Life."

(*Pause.*)

  How famous *am* I?

GIDGER Probably not very. I don't know. I've only found one
  chapter and the index.

JOHN . . . But . . . I'm the *title*!

GIDGER AND I'M NOT *LIST*ED IN THE INDEX!

JOHN . . . I'm sorry, Gidger . . .

GIDGER I quit!

JOHN No, Gidger—

GIDGER I'm going to work for a book that lists me—

JESSIE You can't leave—

GIDGER Oh, and why is *that*, coffee-colored caroler?

JESSIE Because I don't want you going around telling people
  about us—

GIDGER *That's* what you're afraid of?

  You're afraid of *that*?

  Well, let me tell you something: I'm o*ffen*ded!

  By the end of this century, being offended will be the

noblest thing a person can aspire to, and I am pio*neer*ing being offended.

I am in the avant-*garde* of taking umbrage.

Do you think just because I have no history, I have no character?

I'm the most loyal cypher who ever lived!

If I *have* ever lived.

(*indicating manuscript*)

Which, apparently, I have *not*.

JESSIE Then help me burn this office down.

(*Pause.*)

JOHN Jess—

JESSIE Help me make a bonfire—

GIDGER John—

JESSIE Help me incinerate these pages—

JOHN Jessie, they're *books*—

GIDGER The colored races are attracted to fire, John—

JOHN What good will it do—

JESSIE Then we can start over—

GIDGER They burn whole cities and walk away with TV sets—

JOHN Shut up, Gidger—

GIDGER I READ IT IN A BOOK!

JESSIE We start all over—

JOHN That doesn't happen—

JESSIE We know nothing—

GIDGER —'bout birthin' no babies— Where did *that* come from?

JOHN Shut up, Gidger!

GIDGER I WILL NOT BE SILENCED! Oh, right—I will—

JESSIE We know nothing that we don't already know—

JOHN But this is—what *happens*—what else is there?

JESSIE *My* book.

You start up again. You publish my book—it's the only book—all these others—vanish—

(Beat.)

GIDGER *(turning to the index)* Well, let's just see if that happens, shall we?

(JESSIE knocks the pages out of GIDGER's hands. They scatter.)

LOOK WHAT YOU'VE DONE!

(He drops to his knees, starts gathering.)

JESSIE . . . John?

JOHN What don't you want me to know?

(Pause.)

JESSIE *(a plea)* John . . . ?

(Beat.)

JOHN Do you have things to do . . . with your day? I know you have . . . such busy days.

JESSIE *(defeated)* . . . Yes.

All right. Yes.

(She starts to go.)

JOHN Don't forget the theater.

JESSIE . . . I'm sorry?

JOHN We're going to the theater tonight.

JESSIE . . . Oh.

Yes.

JOHN The play . . . I hear it's . . .

JESSIE . . . What?

GIDGER *(from his knees)* Predictable.

(Lights.)

(A late-afternoon light, richly colored.)

(The machine ticks low in the next room.)

(Through the open doors, we can glimpse GIDGER *reading.)*

*(*JOHN *sits on the floor amidst a tumulus of pages, looking vaguely like the Count of Monte Cristo.)*

(He is holding some pages in his hands. His hands tremble.)

JOHN Letter to John Pace Seavering from Denis McCleary. Dated 12 June 1936.

*(*DENNY *appears, pale and sick and older. As he speaks,* JOHN *silently reads.)*

DENNY Dear John:

How sad it must make you to see my return address on an envelope these days! Sorry about that.

Rosamund is home for an extended weekend. Her doctors have been encouraged by her progress this month and think that time spent in what they call a "family atmosphere" might hasten her recovery.

JOHN Recovery . . .

DENNY *(overlaps)* The first night went pretty well—we spoke softly to each other, and the old ugly turbulence was nowhere to be seen. Rosamund is very thin now, and her eyes, though faded in color, look enormous in their sockets, so that even when she's trying not to attack, she seems to be aggressing upon you.

The trouble is, Pace, there's so much history between us now that none of our gestures are innocent, they all *seem* to mean, even when there's nothing to them, even when they don't happen at all.

Meanwhile, I'm trying to hack out a few stories, but this business of being on the wagon—I'm strictly limiting my intake to white wine with lunch, red wine with dinner, and a single cognac before bed—*is not inspiring*, and all I seem able to do is remember. Do you know what I keep thinking of, John?

The first day of April 1919.

JOHN *(overlaps on "1919")* The first day of April 1919.

DENNY You've probably forgotten all about it.

(JOHN laughs, one note, helpless.)

Something that happened in your office—that first suite of offices you had, remember? All crannied and irregular and way high up, and the light slipped in through crevices and made kaleidoscope shapes on the tilting walls.

You had just moved in —there were stacks and stacks of pages around, manuscripts, I guess, that other idiots like me had submitted—and there you were, this preposterous child suddenly granted the power to change men's lives, and mine was the life that most needed changing, and you were the only one who could do it.

And you refused.

I had given you *The Violet Hour*, and you had decided that you couldn't do what you *had* to do for me, which was publish it.

You gave us the news, then went off somewhere, and Rosamund and I were left alone in your office.

, I, for want of a future, was about to lose her to someone undeserving—and without her I didn't want to live —and to my amazement! —*she* didn't want to live without *me*. And so we decided to die for each other . . .

We didn't die for each other, of course; instead, we're dying *of* each other . . .

JOHN Editor's note:

Here there's a gap in the page, and when the letter resumes, the handwriting becomes jagged and indecipherable in places.

DENNY John:

This is being written eight hours later.

Rosamund's bad again. While I was writing this, I heard a noise from the kitchen. I went in to indecipherable and saw her poised over the sink. She was holding a knife and a quantity of blood was gushing from her arms. I tried to indecipherable and either deliberately or not, she ended up slashing at my cheek with her knife—seventeen stitches were sewn; the scar will be ugly.

Eventually I quieted her—I had to indecipherable, I'm afraid—and called an ambulance, which cost twenty-five dollars. She's back at the hospital. I returned home just a few minutes ago, nursing my outraged cheek for which the painkillers I've been prescribed are doing very little. The three fingers of gin seem to be having a salutary effect, at least.

JOHN No—I can't keep—

DENNY *But John, this is what I really meant to be writing you about!*

*(*JOHN *reluctantly goes back to reading.)*

DENNY I'm wondering, as a sort of tide-over while I'm working on the new novel, if you'd consider putting out an edition of some of the earlier stuff. *The Violet Hour* might be able to draw attention as a period piece—there's tremendous interest in that era now—and I really believe that if people were reminded of how good I used to be, they'd receive me better *now*, which, honestly, matters to me as much as any revenue the books might produce, as I have *no interest in posthumous acclaim*!

JOHN Denny—

DENNY *(overlaps on "Denny")* John, what I hate is her laugh.

　　When we're together, she launches that laugh at me pretty much on an hourly basis, and it's become a kind of code.

　　What it says is: You are no kind of a man. My unhappiness is infinite, you are its cause. My hatred for you is indecipherable, may you fry in it.

　　She laughs, then looks at me with that gaze which, when we were young, was all candor and freshness, and now is pure punishment.

　　In the old days, when she felt this madness coming on, she'd secretly rent a hotel room—

JOHN —a hotel room—!

DENNY and hide away in it until she'd squelched herself and was fit to return to people.

Maybe if our money hadn't vanished and her family hadn't lost everything in the Crash, things would still be all right. Maybe the only thing separating us from contentment is the price of a hotel room—

Oh, John, I wish I didn't feel this constant guilt!

JOHN *Stop!*

DENNY That day in April, when Rosamund and I thought we were going to die together, you suddenly reversed yourself—it was a kind of miracle—you said, yes, you'd publish *The Violet Hour*—and our happiness seemed complete.

That book was the making of us both, Pace, and it's all gone well for you, and I'm glad of that . . . but I wish you'd never published it.

I wish the whole thing had never happened . . .

(Lights fade out on him.)

(JOHN looks up, stares straight out.)

(A long moment. Then ROSAMUND *appears in the doorway.)*

ROSAMUND Hello.

(JOHN starts, makes a fright sound.)

ROSAMUND Don't be startled; it's only Rosamund . . .

JOHN What do you want? What do you want?

ROSAMUND Are you quite well?

JOHN . . . Yes.

ROSAMUND Is something wrong?

JOHN . . . No.

No, no.

When people come at me—

(GIDGER enters.)

GIDGER Miss Rosamund Plinth, of the beef-buck Plinths.

JOHN Yes, Gidger—

GIDGER I was in the *toi*let, if you want to know the truth—

That's why the announcement was de*layed*, if you want to know the truth—that's something you won't find in your *chron*icles—things happen because someone's in the *toi*let—

JOHN Please leave, Gidger—

GIDGER . . . Perfectly all right.

I don't need to see the movie, I can just read the book . . .

(He exits.)

ROSAMUND Funny little man.

JOHN Gidger?

ROSAMUND Yes, Gidger. What does he *do*, precisely?

JOHN He helps me out.

ROSAMUND Is it a job with much chance for advancement?

JOHN . . . No.

ROSAMUND Hm. Sad, really.

What will become of him, I wonder?

JOHN I have no idea.

ROSAMUND Is Gidger his first name or his last?

JOHN I DON'T KNOW!

(Startled beat.)

. . . Why are you here?

ROSAMUND That was terribly unfair of me, leaving you the way I left you.

I felt it was terribly unfair of me.

JOHN How you . . . left me . . . ?

ROSAMUND On that note of melodrama . . .

You worried about me . . .

JOHN Yes . . . no.

ROSAMUND Yes, you did, you did.

You left messages all over town, everywhere I stay there was a message.

That was terribly sweet.

JOHN I . . .

ROSAMUND You *are* terribly sweet, you young men.

All the ruthless young men.

All tender and hard-boiled—

JOHN Why have you come back?

ROSAMUND To ease your anxiety.

JOHN I don't have any . . . *anxiety* . . .

ROSAMUND Well, you needn't *have* had.

I wasn't going to jump from any high windows before I gave you the chance to prevent it.

They were quite alarmed at the Plaza—

JOHN The Plaza—

ROSAMUND Yes—where I go sometimes—

JOHN Yes: the Plaza—

ROSAMUND . . . Have you ever been?

JOHN To the Plaza?

ROSAMUND Yes, to the Plaza.

JOHN Only for functions.

ROSAMUND . . . *Bodily* functions?

(He looks at her.)

(She laughs, that lovely sound.)

JOHN DON'T MAKE THAT HIDEOUS NOISE!

(Beat.)

    I mean—

ROSAMUND Are you *quite* all right?

JOHN . . . Y-yes.

ROSAMUND Do you need some sort of bromide? Shall I fetch
one for you?

JOHN No.

ROSAMUND Well. Something seems askew.

    . . .

    Anyway, they're terribly nice at the Plaza, and it's the
loveliest place.

    I always rent a hotel room when I want to daydream.

JOHN To . . . daydream?

ROSAMUND Yes.

    That's what I call it . . .

JOHN And do you . . . daydream . . . often?

ROSAMUND Oh, every once in a while.

    Every now and again.

    I just go all private with myself.

    The good thing about a hotel room is it's not where
you live, so when you daydream, there's never any danger
of mistaking it for your life.

    Do you see?

    I recommend it.

    I recommend it highly.

    It's how I've kept my wits about me.

JOHN . . . And did you go there to daydream this afternoon?

ROSAMUND Well, I suppose I did.

RICHARD GREENBERG

But here's the funny thing:

First I'd gone to my place—*my* place, the apartment, you know.

And all the sweet men at the concierge desk breathed this absolute sigh of relief—because you'd flustered them so—

JOHN I didn't mean to—

ROSAMUND Well, that's all right, that's just fine.

It was sweet, their concern.

So I went upstairs, to my rooms, and they . . . the *rooms*, they . . . they didn't . . .

Well, I felt this *day*dream coming on, so I just hied myself to the Plaza where, as you know, I'd already rented a suite.

And they were all stirred up about me, too—really, it was as if all the young men in Manhattan were a chorus line fretting over me . . . like this jazz chorus singing my name in a nervous kind of unison . . .

Nice, really . . .

. . .

Anyway, I was turning from this particular *branch* of the chorus when who should I see?

JOHN Who?

ROSAMUND My father!

JOHN Your father?

ROSAMUND Can you *imag*ine?

JOHN My—

ROSAMUND He'd come to town without telling me, bad man, and here we were together by sheer coincidence . . .

Well, there's nothing less *dreamy* than a Chicago
meatpacker, so that was that for my daydreaming . . .

JOHN . . . Is it possible to stop them once they start?

ROSAMUND . . . The—

JOHN The daydreams—can you stop them?

(Hesitation.)

ROSAMUND Oh yes, of course.

(Hesitation.)

So he took me to the Palm Court, we had tea.

And I thought of your idea . . .

JOHN My—?

ROSAMUND What you suggested.

About waiting.

About upending all our plans and waiting just a year.

JOHN A year . . .

ROSAMUND Yes, a year . . .

I thought it was providential, you see.

His being here for one purpose, and my being here for
quite another purpose, and you having made your
suggestion—I thought it all made a triangle—a
providential triangle.

So.

I was very endearing.

JOHN I'm . . . sure . . .

ROSAMUND Well, I can be, I can be.

Especially in the Palm Court, where the afternoon
light's all lemon and rose beige.

I said, "Daddy, please may I marry?"

JOHN Marry Denny?

RICHARD GREENBERG

ROSAMUND Yes, marry Denny.

> I said, "Daddy, please may we have another year?
>
> "May we please go back to Chicago together, you and I,
> Daddy, and break a contract and a heart?
>
> "*Both* of which will mend.
>
> "Because I'm in love.
>
> "I'm in love, Daddy . . . and it's what I want to do."

JOHN It's what you will do.

ROSAMUND No! I was . . . gentle.

> I was appeasing.
>
> I said it's what I *want* to do.

JOHN It's what you will do.

ROSAMUND I *pro*mise you, it was a moment from Puccini!

(that silvery laugh)

JOHN DON'T MAKE THAT NOISE!

(She looks at him.)

ROSAMUND Would you like to borrow my room at the Plaza?

> One can be so . . . marvelously alone there.

JOHN . . . No . . . thank you.

> . . .
>
> What did your father say?

ROSAMUND You were right about him.

> He *is* a wicked man.

JOHN He refused you?

ROSAMUND Yes.

JOHN He's not a wicked man.

ROSAMUND Oh?

JOHN He's a wise man.

ROSAMUND Are you mocking me?

JOHN No.

ROSAMUND I think you are—

JOHN You should listen to your father—

ROSAMUND I think you *are* mocking me—

JOHN I'm not—I see things differently now.

ROSAMUND . . . You see them the wrong way.

JOHN Marry the fellow in Chicago, have a life there—

ROSAMUND Publish Denny's book.

(Beat.)

JOHN I—

(Long pause.)

No.

(Pause.)

ROSAMUND I knew you wouldn't.

JOHN How—did you know?

ROSAMUND The curse of prophecy, remember?

Tell me: is it because you want him for yourself?

JOHN . . . No—

ROSAMUND People have told me—

JOHN They've—

ROSAMUND People have sug*ges*ted—

JOHN There are things—

ROSAMUND —over these little tables at these little bars, of course, people will say things—

JOHN Things I've learned—

ROSAMUND —you dismiss them, of course.

But should you?

Maybe you shouldn't.

RICHARD GREENBERG

(And she smiles, and it's a sweet smile but there's something else going on with it.)

JOHN And that's the look that will annihilate him for years.

(Pause.)

(DENNY rushes in.)

DENNY Darling—

ROSAMUND Did you look for me? Did you get my message?—

DENNY I've been so worried—

(GIDGER enters.)

GIDGER Mr. Denis McCleary, unpublished Irish-American author and aspiring dypsomaniac.

JOHN All right, Gidger, thank you—

ROSAMUND Did they tell you?—Did they give you my message?

GIDGER John, I'm reading something—

DENNY I went to the Biltmore—

ROSAMUND I left you a message—you must have re*ceived*—

DENNY Eventually—

GIDGER John—this thing I'm reading—I think you should take a look at it—

JOHN *Later*, Gidger—

GIDGER *(leaving, quiet)* All right, John.

ROSAMUND I told them to seek you out—I told them to look for an anxious young man who's probably pacing—

DENNY It was the Biltmore—that described about thirty people—

Why are you here . . . what's the matter?

ROSAMUND I'm afraid it's all over, darling.

DENNY . . . Over?

ROSAMUND Mr. Seavering won't be publishing your book.

Everything's over . . .

(Pause.)

DENNY What . . . have . . . you . . .

Why not?

JOHN Denny—

DENNY You have to, Pace . . . it's . . . the thing's in *crates*—

No one else will touch it . . .

You said . . . You *pro*mised that—

JOHN I never did, really . . . You just imagined I did.

You're such an optimist, Denny . . . You take what you

hope will happen for what *will* happen.

I can't publish your book.

I'm sorry.

DENNY . . . Do you know what this will mean—?

JOHN Yes—no—

DENNY Do you know what this will mean to us—?

JOHN I know that if I published it—

DENNY This means—

JOHN —it would be catastrophic—

DENNY Oh? You *know* that—?

You've had a *vi*sion?

JOHN . . . In a way.

DENNY . . . You *shit*!

ROSAMUND *(softly)* Denny, please, don't use language—

JOHN *(overlaps)* If I tried to tell you—it would be—

DENNY I *know* what this is—

JOHN It would be—Cassandra—

DENNY I know why you're doing this—

JOHN You're so full of your own destiny, you couldn't
possibly believe anything other than—

DENNY *(overlaps)* This was always in the works, wasn't it?

ROSAMUND Be quiet now, please—

DENNY From the second you clapped eyes on me—-

JOHN This is a sacrifice for me, too—

DENNY *(overlaps)* From the *in*stant you saw me, you
wanted to undo me—

JOHN That's nonsense, Denny—

DENNY *(overlaps)*—because everything I have is *mine*, and
everything you have is inherited—

JOHN *(overlaps)* I can't make you understand—

DENNY *(overlaps)* This—this *friend*ship—this *mockery*—

ROSAMUND Denny—

DENNY This se*duc*tion—

ROSAMUND Denny, please be quiet, please be good—

DENNY What else can you call it?

The way you pursued me—hunted me down in
college—God knows what you really wanted!

It's always the same, isn't it? With you . . . with all of
you. You rich boys.

With your *hon*or . . . and your charity. Your noblesse
oblige!

You woo . . . and *promise* . . . and *weigh* . . . and, at
the moment when nothing else is possible for us . . . you
abandon.

Because there's only one thing that really interests you—and that's making sure that you prevail . . . and we succumb.

Well. It's happened, John.

You've done it.

Congratulations.

(JOHN *approaches him.*)

JOHN Denny—

DENNY DON'T COME NEAR ME!

(*Beat.* JOHN *steps back.*)

(GIDGER *enters.*)

GIDGER John, I'm sorry to interrupt—but I've found something I think you need to see . . .

JOHN Well . . .

. . .

Well . . .

. . .

. . .

It seems there's something else that needs my attention.

I'll . . .

. . .

Each of us is certain he knows how things will end, Denny. The only difference is, I'm right.

I don't know if there's anything I can alter . . . but I *can* refuse to acquiesce.

I can do that much.

. . . You can . . . stay in the room awhile, if you like . . .

(*He takes a step to leave.*)

RICHARD GREENBERG

This book . . . or whatever it is . . . of yours . . . is a marvelous thing, Denny.

I only hope for your sake no one ever publishes it.

I only hope for your sake you die old and obscure.

(He exits, followed by GIDGER.*)*

*(*DENNY *and* ROSAMUND *are alone together.)*

*(*DENNY *looks upset with himself, regretful.)*

DENNY . . . I wonder if I meant any of that.

*(*ROSAMUND *sits on the window ledge, poised—posed— beautifully, looking at him.)*

(The afternoon light has begun to wane; the twilight colors are starting to fill in.)

ROSAMUND Darling.

DENNY . . . Oh God, Rosie . . .

ROSAMUND Saying all that . . .

DENNY Oh God . . .

ROSAMUND . . . whether you meant it or not . . .

DENNY I feel so awful . . .

ROSAMUND . . . there was no point.

What was the point?

(He goes to her, kneels before her. She holds his head.)

Oh, my boy . . .

DENNY . . . What can we do?

ROSAMUND There's nothing to be done.

DENNY How can that *be*?

ROSAMUND We're caught between two willful men.

The world belongs to willful men.

Nothing to be done, darling . . . nothing to be done.

(Beat.)

(She smiles.)

DENNY What if we stopped wanting what they have to give us?

ROSAMUND We'd have to be rechristened . . . we'd have to call each other by different names!

DENNY I don't care about the money—

ROSAMUND No, it's not the money, exactly.

DENNY The hell with their money—

ROSAMUND —it's not the money . . . it's the aftermath.

DENNY After . . . what?

ROSAMUND After . . . *this*.

> After *this* . . . subsides . . . and things become daily.
> If they haven't gone well.
> And the tally starts of what we've lost and what we've stolen from each other.
> The reassurances won't matter then . . . and the excuses won't wash . . . and all the grievances will be ducated away for when we can really use them—

DENNY Why does it have to be that way?

ROSAMUND Because it does.

DENNY Why do we have to *know* it?

> If only we didn't *know*.
>
> . . .
>
> Then the book is the only thing that could save us?

ROSAMUND Yes.

DENNY But it *won't*.

ROSAMUND No.

DENNY . . . And do you *really* go back to Chicago and *actually* marry that man?

ROSAMUND I don't know.

Somehow I can't imagine it.

But what else?

. . .

I wish I'd never met you.

(He looks at her, pained.)

If there has to be more life . . .

. . .

If there has to be every day, and you not in it . . .

. . .

Before, I didn't mind so much that nothing mattered . . .

. . .

Now . . .

(She turns away.)

(In this light, there's something formal about the pose, not self-conscious or insincere, but noticeable to us, almost subliminally. It's like a painting or a photograph.)

DENNY God . . . you look so beautiful . . .

ROSAMUND *(wryly)* It's a trick of the light . . .

DENNY You look so beautiful sitting there . . .

. . .

. . .

Sometimes life is so complete . . . you don't . . .

ROSAMUND *(whispers)* Denis . . .

DENNY . . . I was walking along before . . . on the street . . . when I thought my life had just changed, for the better and for always, I was walking to meet you, because that had been our plan . . . and our bigger plan was in place . . . and the happiness of that . . . was ex*cru*ciating.

I didn't think I could take another moment of it.

I thought: A lifetime of this will ruin me, my lungs can't take it, my heart—!

. . . When I got to the Biltmore, and waited, and you didn't come . . . I knew something bad had happened, something had gone terribly wrong. And that was a hideous feeling, but . . . tolerable somehow.

Somehow I could tolerate that.

(Beat.)

But still, I don't want any *kind* of "aftermath" . . .

I don't want anything *after* this . . .

(Beat. He considers her.)

It *is* the light . . .

(Beat.)

Sometimes happiness is so complete that . . .

(Beat.)

Sometimes the world is so beautiful you don't need any more of it.

You don't need time . . . and money . . . and getting famous, and more time; you want . . . only a gesture . . .

Something so gorgeous it matches the world . . .

. . .

You . . . in this light . . . and you *love* me . . . !

It's enough.

It would be enough.

(Pause.)

ROSAMUND Would it?

(Pause.)

DENNY Yes.

(Pause.)

ROSAMUND I have a room in the Plaza.

. . .

(DENNY looks surprised.)

Sometimes I do that . . . when the places I live get too small and familiar.

I take a wonderful room in a wonderful hotel . . . high up in the sky.

Where I can daydream . . .

The things that make other things impossible . . . vanish . . . in those high rooms . . .

This room I have in the Plaza—it's on the fourteenth floor.

The city's all towers from that window; the towers are all medieval.

And the funny thing? There's no gravity anywhere.

You step off the ledge . . . and you *rise*!

High . . . high . . . high to heaven!

. . .

We could go to the Plaza. We could go there now. I'm on fine terms with the desk clerks . . . and the bellhops . . . and the house detective considers me above reproach. We could go there and have a drink apiece . . . or many . . . and ride the elevator to the fourteenth floor . . . and step together straight into the sky!

It would be the *most* gorgeous gesture.

. . .

Don't you think?

DENNY *(barely a whisper)* . . . Yes.

(They hold each other very tightly.)

ROSAMUND You *are* the only thing in the world I've ever *ever* loved, you know.

(A moment.)

*(*JOHN *enters, disturbed about something.)*

JOHN I'm—oh—I'm sorry.

I—somehow—didn't realize you were still here—I had to get out of the other room—the papers—I was— inundated—

DENNY John.

JOHN . . . Yes, Denny?

DENNY I'm sorry.

I'm sorry for what I said before.

JOHN Thank you, Denny.

I wish things could be different, but—

DENNY No . . . this is better.

(to ROSAMUND*)*

Isn't it?

ROSAMUND Yes.

DENNY This is much more what we want . . .

Thank you, John . . .

JOHN *(mystified)* All right, Denny—

DENNY Thank you for it . . .

JOHN . . . You're welcome . . .

*(*JESSIE *enters.)*

JESSIE Am I early?

*(*GIDGER *enters.)*

GIDGER Miss Jessie Brewster . . . John.

JOHN Yes, Gidger.

JESSIE We've all assembled again . . .

DENNY . . . Yes . . .

ROSAMUND . . . How funny . . . !

JOHN Hello, Jessie . . .

JESSIE . . . We were to meet before the theater . . . Am I
  early?

JOHN *(quiet, complicated)* No, you're right on time . . .

ROSAMUND We're just going— Oh.

   There isn't a *cam*era anywhere, is there? Do you have
   a camera?

JOHN . . . No.

ROSAMUND Oh.

   I thought there should be a picture.

   You should all have a picture.

(Beat.)

   Well.

   Denny and I are going.

   Aren't we, Denny?

(Beat.)

DENNY Yes.

*(*ROSAMUND *starts off,* DENNY *follows.)*

ROSAMUND *(with her back to us, exiting)* Good-bye to
  you all . . .

(They're off.)

*(*GIDGER, JOHN, *and* JESSIE *remain.* JOHN *has picked up
a pack of text pages. He is fiercely concentrated
on* JESSIE.*)*

GIDGER . . . You should ask me to leave, John . . . Don't you
 want me to leave?

JOHN Yes, Gidger, please leave.

(GIDGER goes.)

(A moment.)

JESSIE We were going to get drinks . . . didn't we say
 that?

> We were going to find a place . . . and have a
> cocktail . . .

(Beat.)

> A cocktail before the theater . . . we have to hurry . . .
> to find a place that will be happy with us both . . .

(Beat.)

> A drink . . . or two . . . to make the play bearable,
> ha ha!

(He looks at her. Silent.)

> You shouldn't really look at me that way, John, you
> shouldn't stare . . . It's not nice to stare . . .

(Beat.)

> . . . What have you . . . have you *learned* something
> . . . what is it you've . . . learned . . .

(Beat.)

> Don't be silent, it's not fair to be silent, that's all you
> have to do and you win, you have . . . that power, it's
> not *fair* . . .

(Beat.)

> SAY SOMETHING.

(Beat.)

JOHN You lied.

RICHARD GREENBERG

JESSIE . . . What have you got there?

JOHN You lied to me . . .

JESSIE Have you found another book?

 —another wretched book—?

JOHN How could you *do* this—

JESSIE What have I done? What have I done? I don't know
 what you mean—

JOHN How can you *not* know what I mean—

JESSIE I haven't the least idea what—

JOHN You've *lied*!

JESSIE *Which lie?*

(Beat.)

JOHN Are you white?

(Beat.)

JESSIE John.

JOHN Are you a white woman?

JESSIE Look at me, John: am I a white woman?

JOHN I don't know . . . I can't tell any more. The light in
 here—

JESSIE No, John. I am not a white woman.

JOHN Were you *ever*?

JESSIE How can that be?

JOHN Did you *live* as if—

JESSIE Yes . . . for several years I did.

 For several years in Paris, it seemed a good idea—

JOHN That's not in your book—

JESSIE I met a man there. He said to me, "Have you traveled
 much since you've been in Europe? Have you been to
 your family's home, have you been to the home of your

ancestors?" I didn't know what he meant, he saw I was puzzled, he said, "Well, you're Basque, are you not? *Une basque*."

And I said, "Yes."

JOHN It's not in your—

JESSIE "*Oui. Je suis basque.*" I was speaking French so I thought it might be true—

JOHN It's not in your book—

JESSIE —but it wasn't me—

JOHN It's *not* in your *book*

JESSIE *That* wasn't the truth; the book is—

JOHN May I see your arms?

(Pause.)

JESSIE No.

JOHN I've seen them before.

JESSIE Not the way you mean to look at them now.

JOHN I didn't understand before—I didn't know what I was looking for—

JESSIE You don't have to now—

JOHN I didn't understand these things before—

JESSIE Be quiet now, John—

JOHN I've never understood anything—not a single thing—

JESSIE You understand what matters—you understand what *is*—

JOHN LET ME SEE YOUR ARMS!

JESSIE That was all very long ago—

JOHN But it's *not*—

JESSIE Ages ago—

JOHN You said there's no such thing as time—

JESSIE You do these things—not for pleasure—but to stop
the pain—it's *done*—

JOHN It's not in the book—

JESSIE That wasn't *me*—the book is *me*—

JOHN You—

JESSIE —with everything false burned away—

JOHN *Let me see your*—

JESSIE That's *over*—it's nothing—it should never have been
discovered—there's nothing to discover—I fought it—I
won—why should it be remembered?

JOHN YOU *DIE* FROM IT!

(Pause.)

JESSIE No.

JOHN Eleven years from now—

JESSIE . . . No—

JOHN You've been missing five years—

JESSIE No—*no*—that's not me—that's *you*—
That's all you can imagine for me—

JOHN *(overlaps)* They find you in some horrible little
room—

JESSIE *(overlaps)* That's all you can think of for me—you—
OFAY, you—ENEMY—

JOHN *(overlaps)* On upper Broadway—

JESSIE But I conquered that—I *triumphed* over that—

JOHN *(overlaps)* You've been dead, they think, for a week—

JESSIE *I can't go there from here!*—

JOHN *(overlaps)*—it's hard to tell—your body's started to
decompose, they can't pry the needle loose from your
arm—

JESSIE *That's . . .* NOT *. . .* TRUE!

(She lunges at him.)

   That's not true—that's not true—that's not—

(She's beating on him with her fists. He grabs her and she sinks to the floor, raging and crying. He goes down with her, first subduing her, finally just holding her.)

(They stay together like that. A long moment.)

*(*GIDGER *enters with a manuscript.)*

GIDGER My *dog . . .* becomes *famous.*

(Slowly they look at him.)

(He reads from the manuscript.)

   "Among the varied personages that made Arbiter House such a lively place in its heyday, one was not a person at all but a dog—a universally beloved canine named Sir Lancelot."

*(*GIDGER *looks up at them, goes back to reading.)*

   "Sir Lancelot, who apparently belonged to a woman . . ."

*(*GIDGER *looks up, goes back to reading.)*

   ". . . to a woman who worked briefly at the firm in its early years . . . as a functionary . . ."

*(*GIDGER *looks up, reads again.)*

   ". . . was noted for his noble mien, delightfully antic disposition, and upright character . . .

   "A mix of collie and chow, he also served as inspiration for a goodly portion of the most significant literature of his time . . .

   "His influence was not restricted to Arbiter House authors; the Algonquin Round Table writers also evidenced a marked fondness for the pooch.

". . . In Dorothy Parker's most famous poem, the lines 'Acids stain you' and 'Nooses give' originally read 'Collies *bite* you' and '*Leashes* give' . . .

"When queried as to her reasons for changing the lines, the usually tart-tongued Parker remarked, 'I couldn't live with myself, knowing I'd slandered a character as sterling as that of Sir Lancelot . . .'

"Sir Lancelot, who was legendary for sitting up on furniture like a person, and who was, indeed, considered more human than many human beings, sparked so much love among the notables of his time that each of them called him by a private nickname. Among these were: Lance, Lannie, La, Sir, Siree, Celot, Lut, Ut, Slut, Lot . . . and Lottie . . ."

(Beat.)

*(*GIDGER *silently closes the book.)*

*(*JESSIE *rises, walks to the door.)*

JESSIE . . . Will we be going to the theater tonight, John?

JOHN No, Jessie, I don't believe we will.

(Beat.)

*(*JESSIE *walks to the anteroom.)*

JESSIE May I stay here just a moment, John?

I have to think what to do with my evening.

JOHN Of course.

*(*JESSIE *stands in the anteroom, near the edge of the machine that we can glimpse. We see her in silhouette, thinking. It's a pose, a photograph.)*

GIDGER John?

I've been reading this book.

JOHN *(wearily)* . . . Yes, Gidger?
  What now?

GIDGER Why didn't you tell me? Why didn't you tell me you were *lovers*?

JOHN *Must* we rehash that, Gidger?

GIDGER Not *her* . . .

(And he hands JOHN *the manuscript he's been reading.)*

JOHN *(reads)* "Violet Haze: The Secret History of Denis McCleary and John Pace Seavering . . . Arbiter House, 1995."

(He turns the page, reads.)

  "The spark for this book came to me one day when, in my capacity as special lecturer in Rosamund Plinth McCleary Studies at Hampshire College, I came upon the following while rummaging through the Jessie Brewster Archive. It is an entry from a recently rediscovered diary, and it is dated April first, 1919.

  " 'Just visited John in his insane little office. Walked in unannounced and happened upon a curious scene: John sharing a passionate kiss with a handsome but shiftless-looking young man who I later learned is called Dennis McCrory [*sic*]. Must say, I found the scene *most erotic* . . .' "

*(*JOHN *closes his eyes, tilts his head back to where* JESSIE *is standing, but doesn't turn to look at her.)*

  " 'Wonder if we can find a way of including this fellow in our own little adventures from time to time . . .' "

(Beat. He continues.)

"This entry was only the beginning for me.

"Given the imminent demise of print literature . . . "

(JOHN *looks up.*)

". . . it may be difficult for us to imagine a time in which a book publisher could impose greatly on the main culture, but John Pace Seavering managed this feat. It's long been known that the image he so carefully presented to the world was, for the most part, an artificial construct. Beneath the courteous, almost prim, quasi-Victorian facade lurked a will to power and a sense of hegemonic entitlement that people who knew him, particularly underlings, felt contained a near-physical quality of threat."

(*Beat.* JOHN *doesn't understand.*)

"But this diary entry was the first indication that his relationship with Denis McCleary—which has always been construed along mentor/pupil, even father/son lines—contained an erotic component. Certainly there was no hint of this in Jessie Brewster's memoir— but that book merits special status as a rare example of a text that doesn't include even *inadvertent* truth."

. . .

. . .

"As I delved deeper and deeper into the story, evidence grew that the erotic was not merely a strain in the relationship but perhaps . . . the defining . . . factor . . . in . . ."

(JOHN *looks up.*)

This doesn't happen . . .

GIDGER I would have understood, John.

JOHN But . . . it—

GIDGER I, of *all* people, would have—

JOHN I don't believe . . . this happens—

GIDGER But it's in a book.

JOHN But it isn't *me* . . .

(Beat. The machine starts ticking.)

JESSIE No!

(She flees the machine, into the room. GIDGER *goes to the anteroom.)*

JOHN Jessie—

JESSIE I *can't* . . .

GIDGER It's not a book coming out this time, John—

JESSIE I *won't* let it happen—

I *won't let it finish the way you said it does*—

GIDGER It's *theater* tickets—

JESSIE Good-bye, John.

(She exits.)

JOHN Jessie!

(He lurches after her and is stopped.)

GIDGER It's three seats for tonight's performance of *Faintly My Heart*. That's the play you were going to see!

JOHN Gidger . . .

(A sudden noise; a crowd uproar.)

GIDGER What's that?

(He goes to the anteroom window.)

Oh no . . . !

RICHARD GREENBERG

(He rushes in.)

John—it's Miss Brewster—she's jumped—Oh God—Oh
God! There's a crowd around her—we have to *do*
something—

JOHN I can't move—

GIDGER Oh God! John! We have to—you have to *do*
something!

JOHN I can't move. *I can't move.* I CAN'T MOOOOOOOVE!

(The machine's ticking accelerates, gets fearfully loud.)

(The lights in the room blink.)

*(*JESSIE *appears in the doorway.)*

JESSIE Am I early?

*(The noise cuts off. The lights go back to what they
were.)*

(A moment.)

JOHN . . . What?

JESSIE For the theater?

JOHN *(taking a tentative step)* . . . Gidger, what's
happening?

JESSIE This is the hour I was supposed to meet you, is it not?

JOHN . . . Gidger?

GIDGER Oh—oh—sorry!

(takes announcing position)

Miss Jessie Brewster . . .

(looks at her wonderingly)

Lazarus . . .

*(*DENNY *and* ROSAMUND *sweep in with the air of playful
children.)*

ROSAMUND Are we interrupting—?

DENNY Johnny always has time for us, don't you, old man?

ROSAMUND It's just that we were on the street, and we were suddenly overtaken—

DENNY —swept away—

ROSAMUND —by the most extraordinary feeling of delight—

DENNY —so we came to share it with you. Oh look, how strange: the singer's here!

ROSAMUND Miss Brewster—

DENNY That's right, that's right—

ROSAMUND —who is a genius—

JESSIE I accept the compliment—

DENNY Yes, yes, anyway, well, here's what happened—

ROSAMUND We were just walking along—!

DENNY —sort of abstractedly—

ROSAMUND —when we saw this woman standing in front of a dress shop—

DENNY —this gemmed window—

ROSAMUND —this iridescent—

DENNY —this green-blue-gold-vermilion window—

ROSAMUND It was *so*—

DENNY And of course I'm a Bolshevik, but something about the picture she made—

ROSAMUND It was just entrancing—

DENNY Her chin was propped on her finger—

ROSAMUND —and you could tell she was wondering—

DENNY —not wondering, *planning*—

ROSAMUND Yes: planning—every sort of happiness—and it was such a lovely thing—

DENNY —in the late afternoon, in the great city, on the first day of April 1919—

ROSAMUND —to see a lovely young girl, in the hour before evening, pondering the figure she'd cut, on a splendid occasion, in a gorgeous frock, and knowing that happiness can be bought—

DENNY —for a little while, at least—

ROSAMUND *(overlaps on "at least")* For a little while—

DENNY There was a photographer across the street—

ROSAMUND He was there to—

DENNY He was supposed to be—

ROSAMUND He was there to take pictures of that new building going up up up—

DENNY —that new skyscraper—

ROSAMUND But Denny said to him—

DENNY I said—

ROSAMUND He said: "*Not* the building—"

DENNY *(overlaps)* "Not the *build*ing, don't shoot the building—shoot the woman in the window—"

ROSAMUND *(simultaneously)* "—the woman in the window—"

DENNY I gave him a dollar—

ROSAMUND *I* gave him the dollar—

DENNY Well, yes you did, darling—

ROSAMUND I wonder: do you suppose she's still there?

DENNY Deliberating! I wonder if she is—*that* would be pathetic—

JOHN *Is* she, Gidger? . . . Go look, would you?

GIDGER *(crossing to the window)* Yes, I'll look—

DENNY Well, even if she isn't, the photographer gave me his
address—

ROSAMUND He's giving us a copy of the picture—

GIDGER No, John, she isn't there—

DENNY We'll have the picture—we'll memorialize the
moment—

GIDGER *(overlaps on "moment")* Nothing's there, John—

JOHN Nothing.

GIDGER No crowds—no tumult—

JOHN I see—

JESSIE I hate to break this up—

GIDGER No aftermath—

JESSIE But if we're going to get drinks before the theater—

JOHN Then it makes no difference—

DENNY You're going to the theater?

JOHN It makes no difference what I do—it will happen as it
happens. The century will take its course.

DENNY Oh right: that *play.*

GIDGER That's all right, John—there'll be other centuries.

JOHN Who knows? We haven't seen those pages.

DENNY Say! Can we come with you?

ROSAMUND Denny, don't be rude—

DENNY But it would be fun—

ROSAMUND But you hate the theater.

DENNY But I like parties and things you get for free!
Come on, John, can you scare up a couple more passes
for this thing?

JOHN . . . In fact, we have them, don't we, Gidger?

(GIDGER *crosses to where he took the tickets from the machine.*)

GIDGER Yes, they've come.

DENNY Well, then—

JOHN We'll all go—all five of us—

GIDGER *Five* of us?

(GIDGER *counts the room, ends on himself.*)

　　John, do you mean—

JOHN Yes, you, too, Gidger.

　　We'll celebrate.

JESSIE What are we celebrating?

JOHN . . . I'm publishing the book.

DENNY . . . *Which* book?

JOHN Both books.

DENNY Oh, God love you, you're a wonderful man! (*kisses him passionately*)

JOHN Don't *do* that, Denny!

DENNY But you were so dithering about this!

　　How did you decide?

JOHN I like both books . . . and they seem authentic to me in their ways . . . and that's all I can manage, really.

DENNY That's—!

　　But wait!

　　Who wrote the other book?

JOHN . . . Miss Brewster, as it happens.

DENNY Is that *true*?

JESSIE No.

JOHN No?

JESSIE *I* wrote the *book*.

　　You wrote the *other* book.

DENNY *(not nicely)* Well, we'll see about that, won't we?

JESSIE *(answering in kind)* Oh yes—we'll see—*we'll* see—

ROSAMUND Either way, it's wonderful!

DENNY Yes it is—it *is*.

　　John, will you lose your shirt?

JOHN No.

JESSIE Are you sure?

JOHN Yes.

DENNY You're a man of vision!

JOHN *(sadly)* Oh yes.

DENNY I'm going to be published! I'm going to be *married*!

　　I'M SO HAPPY!

ROSAMUND *(laughs)* Sweet darling . . .

DENNY *(goes to* JOHN*)* Oh, Johnny—thank you. Thank you.

　　I know I can be an idiot—and a brute—and a fool—

　　But the thing is, I love the world so much—*so much*—

JOHN Yes, I know that about you.

JESSIE Well, I don't know about you, but *I* would like to get to the theater early for a change—

GIDGER Oh, absolutely. Because eighty years from now, there are going to be signs in the lobby that say WARNING: THIS PLAY CONTAINS CIGARETTE SMOKING, so we don't have a minute to lose.

(Everybody but JOHN *laughs, gaily, as in a twenties play.)*

JESSIE We'd best hurry if we want to have time for cocktails—

DENNY Oh yes, must have cocktails—

ROSAMUND *Must* have cocktails!

JESSIE And then to the theater!

JOHN Yes, let's, everyone . . . you, too, Gidger.

We'll have cocktails, then we'll go to the theater and watch the play . . . and we'll know everything that's going to happen from the moment the maid enters with the bowl of roses . . . but we'll enjoy it anyway, won't we?

We'll find a way.

Hurry! Let's go! We don't want to miss the curtain.

(And as they move to go . . .

the curtain falls.)

(End of play.)